# BILLY BREMNER'S BOOK OF SOCCER

Frontispiece: *Billy Bremner*.

# BILLY BREMNER'S

# BOOK OF

# SOCCER

**PELHAM BOOKS**

*First published in Great Britain by*
*Pelham Books Ltd*
*52 Bedford Square*
*London WC1B 3EF*
*1974*

ISBN 0 7207 0776 5

*Made and printed in Great Britain*
*by Fletcher & Son Ltd, Norwich*

# Contents

*Don Revie.*

# Foreword
# by
# DON REVIE

Billy Bremner and I have been partners in the Leeds United crusade for a long time now, and I suppose I know Billy as well as anyone, and better than most. Captain of Leeds, captain of Scotland ... those words in themselves speak volumes for the ability and the reputation of Billy Bremner, who has also had the honour of winning the Footballer of the Year award.

I read somewhere last season that Billy was 'a rebel who triumphed over his own, explosive temperament ... a footballer with the heart of a gladiator and the face of a choirboy ... a player now at the pinnacle of a career that has been packed with controversy.'

There's more than a mite of truth in that all-embracing summing-up of Billy. I handed him the captaincy of Leeds United – and with it, added responsibility. He shouldered that responsibility as I had hoped he would, and his whole game blossomed as a result.

Billy's football, his role as the leader, his mature attitude towards the game and everyone in it ... these qualities won him renewed admiration: from opponents, from rival managers, from spectators – and from me.

I partnered Billy in his first-team debut against Chelsea at Stamford Bridge, and although I didn't tell him so at the time, I really felt that here was a footballer who would reach the very top. By the time he was twenty, he had played in no fewer than seven positions for Leeds – and I was United's manager.

Now, a decade has passed, and Billy has played more than 700 games for Leeds, whom he has led to just about every honour that the game can offer – and I'm still his manager. So if we don't know each other inside-out now, then we never shall do.

Scotland team managers such as Willie Ormond and Tommy Docherty have described Billy as one of the great

7

*The Morecambe and Revie show – and it's comedian Eric Morecambe, who is also a director of Luton Town, presenting Leeds manager Don Revie with a gallon of Scotch, which went with the manager of the month award.*

leaders in the game, and I have no hesiattion in going along with that view. Stoke manager Tony Waddington said Billy was 'a perfect example of a player who is deeply involved, and who has sorted things out for himself.'

What Leeds United have achieved, they have achieved as a team, and Billy would be the first to say this, and the last to dispute it. But there can be no argument that his career and the success of Leeds United have run parallel, and that he has played a major role in the scheme of things. In this book, Billy Bremner tells you himself about Leeds United and about his team-mates at

Elland Road; he tells you about his pride in playing for Scotland, and leading them in a World Cup campaign. There are stories by other stars in the world of soccer, and just about every aspect of the game is covered, so there is something to interest everyone, young and old, no matter which team they support or where they live.

I'm delighted to have been able to set the scene for what follows, and I hope and believe that you will thoroughly enjoy reading the contributions of all the famous names in the pages which follow. Not least, of course, the stories recounted by Billy Bremner.

8

(Above): *A salute to the supporters from the Leeds United players before the game gets underway.* (Below): *Down the line goes Billy Bremner, playing host as Scotland's team captain, as he introduces the players to Lord Harewood, president of the F.A., before the game against England.*

*Shake . . . and Scotland skipper Billy Bremner greets England captain Bobby Moore.*

Not only is Billy Bremner one of the greatest players that has ever lived; if ever I were in the front line of a war, he is the man I would most like alongside me.

*FOOTNOTE: As this book was going to press, the news was made public that Don Revie was leaving Leeds to take charge of the England international team. Obviously, everyone at Elland Road was sorry to see 'The Boss', go, after so many happy years of serving under him. But that's football – Don Revie accepted a new challenge, and I wish him every success – except when England come up against Scotland! Thanks, boss, for all the kind words you've said about me . . . and I'm delighted to return the compliment.*

BILLY BREMNER.

# The Team
# behind The Team

Leeds United manager Don Revie – the man we all call 'The Boss' at Elland Road – has said more than once that a manager is only as good as his team. And I don't think anyone would argue that we have proved we have a pretty good team at Leeds. But I think, right at the start, it would be a good thing to return the compliment, and point out that all the players, without exception, have a very high regard for the team that the fans don't see in action on match days . . . the backroom team which has been responsible for guiding us to so much success on the field of action.

At the head of that backroom team, of course, is 'The Boss', himself a famous player in his day, when his career spanned five clubs: Hull City, Leicester City, Leeds United, Manchester City and Sunderland. You may be too young to remember . . . or maybe you've forgotten, if you're one of the Dads reading this, but Don Revie was just as big a name as any of the international stars playing to-day. As a player, I suppose 'The Boss' would concede that he reached the peak of his career when he was with Manchester City. It was also one of the times when his playing career took a downward turn, too, for at one spell, he and City weren't hitting it off, and he actually trained alone, while he was waiting for his future to be settled. I don't suppose 'The Boss' will mind, if I mention that some people regarded him as being a bit of a 'rebel' in those days!

There came a time in his career later, when he was in his early days as the manager of Leeds United, when I imagine he regarded me as a bit of a 'rebel', too, for I was the one who was wanting away . . . I was homesick for Scotland, and made no secret of the fact. But that's another story, as we shall see later on in this book.

Not that Don Revie was a trouble-maker, as a player. He did think about the game a tremendous lot, and he did stand up for what he believed to be right. One of the things he believed was that players went on the field to play football, in the best sense of the word; and Don Revie was a footballer who could measure up to the best. Today, we talk about back-four men, midfield men and strikers. In Don Revie's day (and in my early days as a player, too, come to think of it), there were full-backs, wing-halves, inside-forwards, wingers and centre-forwards. And he was one of the best inside-forwards in the game – at Manchester City, they perfected what became known as the 'Revie Plan', which brought the team a great deal of reward and the spectators a great deal of entertaining, exciting football.

The chances were created by pushing the ball around and making space from deep positions, and then – wham! Suddenly, a City player had broken and the ball was in the back of the net. If you look at the F.A. Cup-final teams of almost twenty years ago, you will see that the Wembley contestants of season 1954–55 were Newcastle United and Manchester City. There were some names still revered in football in those sides ... Sunderland manager Bob Stokoe was in Newcastle's line-up, and Don Revie was in the City team. Newcastle won, 3–1, and City trooped off the field disappointed, but vowing that they would be back the following year.

They were, too – and Don Revie was in the side which licked Birmingham 3–1. So he collected a winner's medal. That game was dramatic, because Manchester City's 'keeper Bert Trautmann played on with a broken neck – they said afterwards it was a miracle he had

lived to tell the tale. But he wound up not only with a winner's medal, but with the Footballer of the Year award. And he was the second player in succession from Maine Road to win this award, for the previous season, on City's first Wembley appearance, the Footballer of the Year had been ... Don Revie.

They say that history repeats itself, and it certainly did: because just ten years later, Don Revie managed the Leeds United team which went to Wembley. That side lost, against Liverpool, in extra time. And the Footballer of the Year was Bobby Collins, of Leeds United.

A few years later – in 1967 – big Jack Charlton collected the Footballer of the Year award, and three years after that, it was my turn to make a speech of thanks, after having been honoured in a similar manner. A lot of water had certainly flowed under the bridge since 'The Boss' had won his award.

Eventually, as his playing career drew to a close, he joined Leeds United. And when I made my debut for Leeds, against Chelsea at Stamford Bridge, he was my inside-forward partner when I played on the right wing. It was then that I really came to see, for the first time, just how much this fellow thought about the game – and about other people in it. For he looked after me like a father. We roomed together, the night before the match; he talked to me continuously about the game, and did everything possible to put me at ease. And then he went out and played a blinder – and made sure that I got my fair share of the ball.

*Jack Charlton playing for Leeds United and Bob Latchford, then playing for Birmingham.*

midable assignment. Don Revie became the manager, and suddenly we had to start calling him 'Boss'. He was on trial: he knew it, and we knew it. But he showed once again what a determined fellow he can be, when he sets his mind to it.

Deep down, he cherished an ambition. It wasn't merely to take Leeds United to the First Division. It was to see that Leeds became recognised as THE team in the country. At that time, the glamour club was Manchester United, no doubt about it. 'The Boss' wasn't above going to Old Trafford and having a chat with the manager there, Matt Busby, and getting some good advice about the way he should tackle things at Elland Road. Don Revie also nursed this burning ambition to make sure that, one day, Leeds would take over the mantle of Manchester United . . . and I think few people would argue now that Leeds have become accepted as just about the greatest club in the country. It's taken ten years and more to do it, but we've succeeded, in the end. And I'm sure 'The Boss' feels all his efforts have been rewarded.

But even he didn't do it all on his own, as he would be the first to admit. Of course, the players on the park are the ones who get the results – but there has to be a backroom team to find and groom the players, in the first place, and to assess the strength and weakness of the opposition. Don Review showed his first-class judgment when he picked The Three Musketeers . . . Maurice Lindley, Syd Owen and Les Cocker.

Maurice Lindley does a lot of the

Leeds, at that time, were going through a sticky spell, and it was obvious that there were many things to be done before the club could aspire to winning honours – even promotion from the Second Division looked a for-

'spying' jobs for Leeds United. He travels around the country – and abroad – checking on the teams we are due to play in the coming weeks. He weighs up their strong points, he looks for their weaknesses; and then he comes back to Elland Road armed with a dossier which is used to give us our briefing. I know that many clubs have their 'spies', but I know, also, that not one club in Britain does the job of vetting the opposition more thoroughly than Leeds do. And while I don't intend to give away any secrets, I will say that the information we have been given about opposing teams has helped us on many occasions to collect a point, or even to win a match.

Syd Owen and Les Cocker seem to go together like . . . well, like fish and chips. You don't talk about the one without thinking of the other. And you can take it from me that they are hard task-masters, when they feel the occasion requires it. I've done my share of sweating blood in training sessions under these two guys – and it's been going on for a fair old while, now!

These two fellows don't just put you through the hoop; their constant aim is perfection. It doesn't matter that you're an international with dozens of caps, they will still give you a going-over; and, if you have any sense, you still listen to them, because you know that it's all for your own good, and that you can never stop trying to learn in football. One of the things they have drilled into us is that you don't work just when you're running with the ball – you keep on working when you haven't got it. You

try to find space for yourself, so that the team-mate with the ball can find you with a pass. And you work, work, work every minute of the game, whether Leeds are defending or attacking.

Maurice Lindley started off on the backroom side of Soccer with Crewe. Les Cocker was a player with clubs such as Stockport County and Accrington Stanley, who are no longer in the League. If you look at the F.A. Cup-final teams for season 1958–59, you will see the name of Owen there, in the Luton Town line-up against Nottingham Forest. Like Don Revie, when he played against Newcastle, Syd Owen finished up on the losing end against Forest. Like Don Revie, Syd Owen collected a Footballer of the Year award. And, like Don Revie again, Syd Owen became a manager – with Luton, the club he had served so long and so well as a player.

Syd Owen and Les Cocker first teamed up when Syd was managing Luton, and looking for a trainer. They didn't know each other, but there was something about the letter of application from Les Cocker that struck the right note with Syd. And when the two met, that was it – Owen and Cocker were in business.

One day, Syd Owen had to make up his mind about joining Don Revie at Leeds United. He decided to go to Elland Road . . . and before long, Les Cocker was on the Leeds staff, as well. The pair of them, Syd and Les, have remained faithful to 'The Boss' and to Leeds United, despite the fact that they could have branched out elsewhere more than once. Several years ago, there

*Les Cocker is usually in action tending his own players . . . but this time it's the referee who needs 'running repairs'.*

was a good job going at Tottenham Hotspur, and Syd Owen could have had it for the asking. But he stayed with Leeds. Les Cocker has graduated to international status, as trainer not only of the England Under-23 side, but right-hand man to Harold Shepherdson, who is right-hand man himself in the England set-up.

Like Don Revie, Messrs. Lindley, Owen and Cocker have stayed with Leeds. They began the job together, and they have remained at Elland Road to see it through. And I am sure that all of

them feel that it's been worth while, despite the doubts, at times. And believe me, there HAVE been doubts, in varying degrees and in different ways, among the backroom team and the players, through the years. But somehow, we have resolved all the doubts, we've shrugged them aside, and we've remained a United family.

It's no secret that 'The Boss' himself could have landed jobs several times over during his career at Elland Road. Only a year or so ago, it looked, at long last, as if he might just decide to throw

15

in his hand, and take up a challenge elsewhere. Clubs from abroad have tried to tempt him, as well as clubs in this country – and I suppose it's true to say that if he had gone, Leeds United would have survived.

After we had lost the 1973 F.A. Cup final against Sunderland, we were feeling down in the dumps. Not for the first time, of course, because we had come through similar experiences, such as when we were pipped for the League championship, when we had lost the F.A. Cup final against Chelsea, when we had been knocked out of the European Cup at the semi-final stage, when we had fought our way to the final of the European Cup-winners Cup, only to finish up on the losing end.

Of course, Leeds had also won the League title, the League Cup, the F.A. Cup and the Fairs Cup (twice). But it is in moments of stress and disappointment that people tend to fling failure in your face, and ignore the success you have achieved. They also don't talk about the fact that you've failed because you've been trying to win not one, not two, but three things in the same season.

Always, Don Revie had been there to console us, to make us grit our teeth and determine that we would come back the following season and show the doubters that we were made of the right sort of stuff. And, invariably, we had scored a success to make up for past failure. But last year, somehow, the doubts were not so easily dispelled, for it did appear that our manager might be moving on. And that would have been the most bitter blow of all.

As ever, he had rallied us in our moment of despair, after that Cup-final defeat by Sunderland. But it seemed as if the parting of the ways might be on the cards. And that, in itself, was enough to raise gnawing doubts in the minds of the players. If 'The Boss' went, could we do it all again, this time for someone else? It was as if the family faced being split up, with the No. 1 member taking his farewell.

I make no apologies for saying that the players felt it all so deeply that we talked about it among ourselves, and we talked about it to 'The Boss'. We made it plain that we didn't want to see him leaving Elland Road. I don't know if it was this that did the trick, although I like to think our obvious concern certainly helped him to make up his mind.

But whatever it was which finally clinched matters, 'The Boss' did a great deal of thinking while he took a short holiday abroad, playing golf and working out his future in his own mind. And he announced that he was staying at Leeds, that this was where he felt his future lay – and, once we knew that, the tension was lifted.

I think it was probably then that we became determined to reward him for standing by us. And the best way we knew how was to kick off the season and win match after match. The story of last season now is one for the record books. I believe it showed, better than anything, just what sort of team spirit Don Revie has forged among the United family at Elland Road. For we finished up as the League champions.

# The
# Defenders

*Paul Madeley.*

There are so many famous names, so many international players at Leeds United, that it's difficult to know where to start. So I think now, having told you about the backroom team, I can do no better than introduce you to the lads who make things tick on the field. And while it may seem a little bit odd, to go from back to front, that's just what I will do. Which brings me first to our last line of defence, David Harvey.

Leeds have never been content to play second fiddle to anybody else; but David had to do just that for several years. He was second in the line of succession – and the man in possession was Gary Sprake, who is now with Birmingham. As the weeks and the seasons went by, David Harvey looked – and felt – as if he were the permanent reserve. In fact, he eventually came to the conclusion that the only way for him to get regular first-team football was to move on to another club. So he asked for a transfer.

Leeds reckoned they had the best two 'keepers in the country, at that time, but it seemed that other clubs were a bit reluctant to pay a hefty fee for a goal-keeper who had spent most of his life playing in the reserves. So David, born

17

*David Harvey.*

*Paul Reaney.*

*Gordon McQueen.*

*Norman Hunter.*

*Trevor Cherry.*

*Terry Yorath.*

and bred in Leeds, stayed at Elland Road. And even later on, when he was available again, at around £40,000, somehow a deal never materialised, although one or two clubs were on the verge of paying out the money. Today, David Harvey is a Scotland international, and the No. 1 goalkeeper at Elland Road . . . and there's one other thing for certain: £40,000 wouldn't come even near to buying him!

David is one of the quiet lads, one of the unsung heroes of the game. Sometimes he has a bit of a go at us, because he doesn't get enough work to do! But we know that when he's called upon to make a save, we can rely on him doing his stuff.

He played a few times at Elland Road as a schoolboy, but he admits he never had any notions of becoming a professional footballer. In fact, if you ask him, he'll tell you he went in goal in the first place because he didn't fancy getting thumped by the big lads who played outfield! He wanted to settle for the quiet life. But when he was thirteen, he was invited to go down to Leeds for coaching and training, and there he stuck. At fifteen he signed as an apprentice professional, and at sixteen, he made his debut for the reserves, against the Wolves at Molineux. David still talks about that game – he received an injury to an arm, he pulled ligaments in both knees . . . and Wolves stuck six goals past Leeds.

The next day, Les Cocker, who was treating his injuries, told David: 'There'll be plenty more like that, before you've finished.' And David knows the truth of that forecast well enough, because he was in goal the night West Ham, for whom everything went right, put seven goals past him, in a League Cup-tie.

It took David Harvey more than 200 reserve-team matches . . . and a handful of first-team games . . . before he finally nailed down that spot as a first-team regular. He never got in, unless Gary Sprake was injured, even though he played in the odd European tie against sides such as Partizan Belgrade and Spora, of Luxembourg. He also played in front of 60,000 fans at Old Trafford, against Manchester United, and at Old Trafford again, in front of a full house, when Leeds replayed the F.A. Cup final against Chelsea. He played against Spurs, when they ended a Leeds run of more than thirty games without defeat, and against Liverpool, when they won 2–0 to finish up by taking the First Division championship. And after each occasional appearance, it was back to the reserves for David Harvey.

If ever a footballer played a lone game of patience, it was this lad. Finally, his patience was rewarded, when Gary dropped into the reserves and David was given his chance of an extended run. He grabbed it with both hands, and ultimately it was Gary who moved on, when Birmingham paid Leeds £100,000 for him. In the old days, when he had to play the waiting game, David used to tell himself that Paul Madeley and Terry Cooper faced up to similar problems. And they both made it, in the end.

And, having mentioned Terry, let me

*Terry Cooper in action.*

introduce you to one of the most courageous guys I have ever met in the game. I can tell you that everyone – and I do mean everyone – at Leeds was delighted, when Terry finally came back to the first team, after twenty-one months of near-heartbreak, of agonising doubts about whether or not he even had a future in big-time football any more.

And while I'm at it, let me add that Trevor Cherry epitomised the spirit which exists at Leeds, when he stoutly maintained that if he found he'd lost his place at No. 3, he'd be fighting to stay in the side in some other position! He didn't begrudge Terry his chance of a first-team comeback, but he was professional enough himself to give warning to everyone else that he wanted to be involved in the action, somewhere or other. And it's this sort of attitude which keeps us all on our toes. Trevor, signed from Huddersfield, had done an excellent job at left-back during Terry's absence; but, as Paul Madeley had had to do before him, Trevor was ready and willing to move around, just so long as he nailed down a place in the side.

Ten years ago, Terry Cooper was regarded as a full-back, but he could get into the team only on odd occasions, usually when someone was injured. That seems to have been the story of so many of my Leeds team-mates, at varying times! When we played Swansea, in the match which was to clinch promotion for United, Terry was a shock choice – at outside-left. But, in fact, he had kicked off his career eighteen months earlier as a left-winger, so we all knew what he could do, even though he had come to be recognised as a left-back.

That game at Swansea was Terry's League debut, but it was back to regular reserve football for about a year after that, when he went to Everton 'just for the ride', as he said, when we were playing them in the F.A. Cup. He was a shock choice that night, too, and again it was at outside-left . . . but at half-time, 'The Boss' told Terry to drop back more and keep Everton danger-man Alex Scott, playing on the right wing, quiet. So Terry was see-sawing between left wing and left-back, until he finally made the No. 3 jersey his own.

His experience, of course, helps to explain why he was such a success with England, as well as Leeds, when it came to making the overlap from left-back position and down the wing, as an extra attacker. But then came a game at Stoke in which Terry went down . . . and was carried off with a broken leg. It was a blow to England, as well as Leeds; but Terry suffered more than anyone.

He had an operation; he spent months hauling himself back to the verge of fitness. At first, we used to laugh and joke with him, to jolly him along and tell him to hurry up. But as time went by, we could sense that even Terry was beginning to wonder if his career would come to an end. It was a painful thing to watch him striving to regain total fitness. It was hard for us . . . but it was torment for him. Then he saw the specialist again, and the report was that another operation was needed, this time to graft some bone on to the affected shin. The forecast was that this operation would do the trick. And so it turned out.

But by the time Terry made his comeback – in a reserve-team match at Newcastle last season – almost two years had gone by since he broke his leg at Stoke.

Two years of sheer, hard graft, of pain and a refusal to give in . . . no one, but no one deserved the reward of a first-team place more than Terry Cooper. For he really had done it his way, the hard way. He had missed two F.A. Cup finals, big games at home and in Europe, and international appearances. Some people reckon that had he been playing for England, they would have got to the World Cup finals. I don't know about that, but I do know that Terry scored the goal which won the League Cup for us, in March, 1968 . . . and he might just have done the trick for England. Come to that, he might have scored a few goals which would have enabled us to win more honours, too.

Terry is a Pontefract lad, full of Yorkshire grit – and he's needed every ounce of it, during the past couple of years. He had to suffer a disappointment when he was awarded his first full international cap, too, for he had to drop out of a game against Bulgaria, through injury. It meant that his full-back partner at Leeds, Paul Reaney, got a call-up by Sir Alf Ramsey – and typically, Terry wished Paul all the best, but warned: 'I'll be going flat out to win that cap, as soon as I'm fit!' He did win quite a collection of caps, too, once he was fit, and he would have won many more, but for that broken leg which cut almost two years out of his career.

Now, Terry isn't the only Leeds player to have suffered – Paul Reaney broke a leg, as well, in a match at West Ham. Paul had a long spell out of action too – he used to watch us playing as he sat up on a stretcher, after he sustained

that injury – and when he regained complete fitness, he had to fight to get a place in the first team once more, for Paul Madeley had settled down to the No. 2 spot and was playing so well. But, like Terry Cooper, Paul came back.

The more I look round the Leeds United dressing room, the more I realise what characters – and men of character – we have in our playing squad. Maybe it's a combination of that Yorkshire grit, plus the fact that players have had to overcome tremendous obstacles in the way of injuries, which has helped us as a team and as a club to get right to the top. They say that a true test of a man's character is the way he behaves in adversity, and the same can be said of a team and a club. Individually, and collectively, the players of Leeds United have responded remarkably to the challenges thrown up by adversity. No one can deny this.

Paul Reaney talks as Yorkshire as Terry Cooper, although he was born in London. But since he moved to Yorkshire when he was only a fortnight old, he can really claim to be a Tyke. He played for his school team and his local youth club – one game Saturday morning, the other in the afternoon – and was so busy kicking a ball around himself that he never had time to watch Leeds United. When he signed for us, in October, 1961, he had seen Leeds play only a couple of times.

Since then, he's graduated not only to the first team at Leeds, but to full international status. And, as he sometimes reminds me, when we are arguing the respective merits of England and Scot-

*If you want the ball, you've got to get past me first! That seems to be the attitude of Paul Reaney here.*

23

land, we aren't always on the same side! In fact, he was playing for Young England and I was a member of the opposition, in a match at Aberdeen one night. Fortunately, we finished up honours even on that occasion.

Paul Reaney, Trevor Cherry, Terry Cooper . . . the England–Scotland rivalry . . . so let's meet now the new boy at Leeds United, Gordon McQueen, a young Scot who joined us from St. Mirren something like a couple of years ago now. Gordon had the unenviable job of trying to follow in the boots of big Jack Charlton, who played 600 games for Leeds, and it says much for this quiet young Scot that he has been accepted, not just at Leeds, but outside of football, as the rightful heir to the Charlton throne. Big Jack was an automatic choice at No. 5 for Leeds, through so many years. When it became clear that his days were numbered – and he played until he was thirty-seven – a lot of careful screening had to be done to find his successor. The eventual choice fell upon Gordon McQueen, but it was months before we met him at Elland Road. And Gordon himself admits that there were times he felt he'd never get there, as a deal seemed set, only to fall down again.

As a lad, Gordon played 'anywhere I could, to get a game'. Then he developed as a centre-half, and played for a Scottish junior club called Largs Thistle. He went for trials with Glasgow Rangers and Liverpool, but finally signed for St. Mirren, where the manager at that time, Alex Wright, was a friend of Gordon's Dad. Leeds United watched Gordon McQueen for something like a year, before they finally clinched the signing.

Gordon recalls that he was sitting watching T.V., the night before a Scotland–England match at Hampden. Suddenly, he was listening to a sports reporter saying that he was going to Leeds, for £30,000. That was news to Gordon, so he hurried to the phone, and rang the ground at Love Street. It turned out that the Saints wanted considerably more money than £30,000 to let him go.

The next night, he went along to the international, and he was feeling a wee bit sorry for himself – because there, on the field, he was watching Billy Bremner playing for Scotland and Norman Hunter playing for England. And he was still an onlooker, instead of a teammate. Don Revie himself made two more checks on Gordon, and then, when St. Mirren went to play Norwich in a pre-season game, it seemed that things were falling into place, at last. Gordon was supposed to be signing that night, after the game – but, once more, nothing happened.

And then, one day, he walked into the ground at Love Street to be called into the office and told: 'We've agreed a fee with Leeds . . . you're on your way.' Gordon was over the moon, and hurried to Elland Road at full speed. The signing was completed, and he had the job of proving to everyone that he could fill Jack Charlton's boots. But – of course! – there had to be a snag. Big Jack was playing in the reserves, and helping Gordon sort out his game there, while Paul Madeley was holding down the No. 5 job in the first team. 'The Boss' had

24

*Rising to the occasion . . . that's Norman Hunter, with team-mates Paul Madeley and Billy Bremner in support, against Manchester United.*

told Gordon it would probably be a couple of seasons before he was a first-team regular himself.

But after twenty reserve games, Gordon got his big break. He was due to play in the reserves against Blackburn, but that Saturday morning, an S.O.S. came through from the first-team headquarters at Derby. Eddie Gray was injured, and Gordon had to get down there at once. He hurried to Derby, and made his debut, wearing the No. 11 shirt. It was one which had been worn at various times by various players – Terry Cooper and Paul Madeley among them – and it marked the start of Gordon McQueen's First Division career.

Gordon often says that when he arrived at Leeds, he was glad to receive a warm welcome from the Scottish lads such as myself and Eddie Gray. He also pays a tribute to the help he received from big Jack and from Norman Hunter, the fellow we all call 'Tarzan'. No doubt you've all heard the famous joke that 'Norm bites yer leg' . . . well, Norman Hunter is a hard player, and he's the first to admit it. But what a player to have on your side!

'The Boss' once admitted that when Norman was injured, one season, and out for a fair while, that was the time our chances of the First Division championship began to slip away. Norman Hunter is a key man in the Leeds United side. He has also become a key man for England, and I can tell you we all felt terribly sorry for him last year, after that mistake which cost a goal against Poland, in the World Cup qualifier.

England team trainer Harold Shepherdson tells how Norman came into the dressing-room at the end of the match, when England were out of the World Cup, and said simply: 'I screwed it'. There wasn't anyone who could find it in his heart to apportion blame, and Norman had everyone's sympathy. After he had got bathed and changed, Norman drove home through the night to Leeds, and he was out training early the next day. On the Saturday, he played a blinder, just as he had done for England, that one mistake apart.

Now, when you can put a mistake behind you, and get down to the nitty-gritty again, that's the true hallmark of a supreme professional. And Norman Hunter is a professional, through and through. I think, deep down, he must have been one at the tender age of fifteen, when he first joined Leeds – although, believe it or not, he was another who wanted to get back home, in those early days.

Norman was born at a place called Eighton Banks, and he didn't really settle away from home. In the end, the problem was solved by his Mum going to Leeds to live – and, as well as Norman, she took a couple of other Leeds youngsters under her wing. Norman made friends with Gary Sprake and Paul Reaney, and they stuck together so much that I used to call them Snap, Crackle and Pop. It took Norm just four seasons to nail down a first-team place at Elland Road, and offhand I cannot remember him ever having been out of the side, except on the rare occasions he has been injured. He was an England Under-23 player by the time he was twenty, and is now recognised as an England regular, although he had to wait quite a while to pin down a first-team spot there.

Norman has the reputation of being a bit of a tough guy, but you need more than mere brawn to stay at the top in First Division and international football. You also need more than one foot, even if Norman has just about the most educated left leg in the business. You need stamina, the physical assets to challenge for and win the ball, a footballing brain – and no small supply of ability. Take it from me, Norman has got the lot, including that last commodity. And when he goes down injured and stays down, I'll tell you something else . . . you know he's really been hurt. For he's not one of the play-actors.

# The Men who make us TICK!

*Johnny Giles.*

You've met the lads who put the stopper on opposing attacks. Now let's take a look at the players in the 'engine room' – midfield. I suppose that, immediately, the names of Billy Bremner and Johnny Giles spring to mind. So let's deal with them first. And, as my name is on the cover of this book, I'll take the liberty of writing about myself in a bit of detail here. You might as well get to know me better, without further ado.

I hail from Stirling, and that's north of the Border. My early days were spent in a place called Raploch, which is a pretty hard district. And if you were on the small side, as I was, then you had to punch every ounce of your weight. I was playing for the under-11 team when I was nine; I was playing for an under-21 team in juvenile football when I was thirteen; and in my final year at St. Modan's School I forced my way into the Scotland boys' side. Red hair, a bit of pugnacity ... it helped a bit; and, I like to think, so did the fact that I could play football. I played for Scotland boys against England at Wembley, and our opponents looked like giants, compared with the tiches we had on our side. And after that, I found football clubs were interested in signing me. Arsenal, Chelsea, Glasgow Celtic . . . and Leeds United. I knew little about Leeds, and cared less. But I finished up being impressed enough to decide that they were the club for me. But, having gone there, I soon decided I wanted to get back to Scotland!

Maybe I would have gone, too, if I hadn't been given quick promotion to the reserves. I was still ready to return home when I got into the first team, alongside Don Revie against Chelsea, at Stamford Bridge.

Call it the impatience of youth, call it homesickness, call it what you want. I wasn't enamoured of life in Yorkshire, nor was I sufficiently impressed to feel that Leeds were going up in the world. And even after Don Revie became 'The Boss', I was still hankering after a move back home. In fact, when Hibernian offered £25,000 for me, I was over the moon, as we say. This, I thought, was it. But Leeds stuck out for another £5,000, and the deal fell through.

Around that time, Don Revie must have been fed-up with seeing me in his office, always talking about getting away. I had a girl friend in Stirling, and I was back home as often as I could get there. Finally, 'The Boss' went up especially to see my girl friend, Vicky, and talked to her about me. She talked to me, and I decided to give it a real go

at Leeds, instead of keeping chuntering about moving back home. And the day dawned when Vicky and I were married, and she moved south for us to set up home together in Leeds. What would I have missed, had 'The Boss' given way and told me I could get out and stay out!

So, you see, it wasn't always a love affair between Billy Bremner and Leeds United, even if I did used to baby-sit for Don Revie and his wife, Elsie, in those early days. Now Don's children are grown up, I have a family of my own. And I suppose you could say that Billy Bremner has grown up, too.

I used to get into a fair bit of trouble with referees, usually for shooting off my mouth. 'The Boss' showed once again what a great psychologist he is, because he handed me the captaincy – and with it, of course, the added responsibility. Added to that, I like to think I have matured, and that I can count to ten and even start to smile these days when someone has just kicked a lump out of me. Then again, the gradual and increasing success of Leeds United over the years has made me only too well aware of what I have got, and how valuable it is to keep what I have got. I couldn't be with a greater club, I couldn't play in a finer team. I've been honoured by being chosen as Scotland's captain. And I've won medals and trophies, and played in the World Cup.

Yes, when I look back now, I can see that it's all gone for me, through the years, and I can only add that I'm grateful to 'The Boss' and other people who, at various times, talked sense to me and kept me on the right road. I hope, and I like to think it is so, that I have helped some of the youngsters who arrived at Elland Road after me ... lads like Gordon McQueen, Joe Jordan, Terry Yorath and Mick Bates, among others.

Now there's a point which I think you might find interesting – my midfield partnership with Johnny Giles. Some people ask me – and I know folk have asked him – whether or not we have a sort of mental telepathy going between us. The simple answer is – I don't know.

What I do know is that we have been playing alongside each other for so long now that we seen to anticipate every move. I know what Johnny's going to do, he knows what I'm going to do – and it works, for Leeds United.

Having brought Johnny into the act, let me tell you some more about him. I've known a lot of footballers in my time, but I have never known one remain more modest, or more likeable, in all my years in football. This fellow, a regular Republic of Ireland international

*This is the target area – where the going can get tough. Manchester United's Alex Stepney has to make a point-blank save from Leeds United's Johnny Giles.*

29

– he was made their player-manager last year – still takes the same size in hats as he did when he came over from Ireland as a kid.

I started with Leeds United when we were both at the bottom; Johnny came to Leeds from a club which was at the top – Manchester United. He had just won an F.A. Cup-winner's medal with them; he and Nobby Stiles were brothers-in-law, as well as pals and team-mates; and he deliberately took a step down the soccer ladder, to prove a point.

Johnny hadn't been able to command a regular place or a regular position at Old Trafford. Sometimes he was in, sometimes he was out. Sometimes he played on the wing, sometimes it was at inside-forward. I think Don Revie, who signed him for £40,000, had it in mind that Johnny could be the successor to Bobby Collins, who was our midfield mastermind at the time. I think that Johnny felt he needed a change of club to prove to himself and the world of football that he had the necessary talent to hit the top and stay there.

Johnny went to United as a kid. He once said: 'If you go somewhere as the office-boy, you tend to remain the office boy. It's not that people look at you like that ... maybe it's you who feel like that, and you can't shake it off.' So Johnny left Old Trafford, and gambled his future at Leeds. Like me, he's shared in all our triumphs, collected medals galore and stamped his authority on the game. I wouldn't dispute the claim, either, that he is just about the most accurate passer of a ball in the game – he

can chip and float a pass to perfection, across the field, to the far post or the near post. And drop the ball right on a team-mate's head.

If Johnny Giles felt that he was 'the office-boy' at Old Trafford, Paul Madeley must have felt that he was the odd-job man at Elland Road. For, in his time at Leeds, he's played in just about every position. Not surprisingly, Paul is Leeds United through and through, for he was born within a stone's throw of Elland Road, and his loyalties have always been with the club he supported as a kid. But those loyalties must surely have been tested more than once, in his early days as a United player, for it seemed as if he could get into the first team only because of misfortune to others.

It took Paul quite a while before he had made a regular first-team spot his own – and in the intervening seasons, he had played in no fewer than nine positions. No wonder everyone called him Mr. Versatile. It's a compliment, of course; but I think any player must reach a stage when he wonders where on earth he is going, when he's in and out, and constantly wearing a jersey with a different number.

Paul has always been an unassuming character, but somewhere, deep down, there must have been a streak of steel in his make-up. He admits that he's no racehorse, even today, but right back at the start, there were those who thought that perhaps he wasn't mobile enough to make the grade. Paul simply worked all the harder, to prove the doubters were mistaken ... and how he's succeeded! Now he's an England international.

In fact, Paul played in a representative team which went to Canada, even before he had become a first-team regular at Leeds. And he'd really cracked it when he was given the chance to go with England's squad to the World Cup finals in Mexico in 1970. But Paul – who has always said he didn't mind where he played, so long as he was in the side – said 'No, thanks' on that occasion. He felt he was doing himself, Leeds United and England a service, for at the time he had played almost sixty matches for Leeds, including a spell of eight games in eighteen days. Mr. Versatile had played more games than anyone else in United's team, and he was feeling utterly whacked; so he felt it wouldn't be fair to anyone to undertake the trip to Mexico, and he told Sir Alf Ramsey this, quite frankly. Sir Alf understood . . . and later, he proved he hadn't forgotten Paul.

I suppose Paul is one of those players who will always provoke arguments about which is his best position. Is it at right-back, at centre-half, in midfield? He's made such a success of every job he's ever been called upon to do for Leeds United that it's difficult, if not impossible, to say he's better in one spot than another. This guy is not only Mr. Versatile . . . he's Mr. Reliable. But I think that, overall, perhaps he makes his greatest contribution when he's playing in the middle of the park.

In that sort of situation, he's able to cover a lot more ground. He can defend, he can win the ball, he can distribute it.

*Terry Yorath.*

He can drop back to cover, he can add strength to the midfield. But the fact remains that he's a 90-minute man WHEREVER he plays, and he has the talent to slot into any position as if he'd been born to play there. You cannot pay a professional footballer greater tribute . . . so I'll leave it at that, and move on to two more men who have shown they

31

can match up to the best, whenever they have been called into the first team. Meet Terry Yorath and Mick Bates . . .

Terry comes from Wales, and he went to a Rugby-playing grammar school down there. He was invited for trials at scrum-half with Cardiff Boys – and

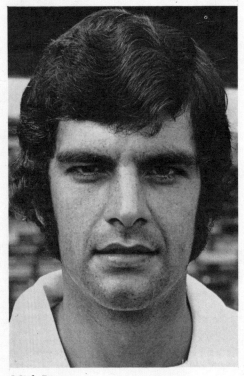

*Mick Bates.*

finished up playing soccer for the city boys. Terry's brother had been picked to play at soccer, and Terry was there to watch him, until it turned out that Cardiff were a player short. So Terry borrowed a pair of boots, and got cracking.

After that first outing at soccer, Terry

was brought into the squad, and collected four Welsh schoolboy caps as a left-winger, playing in the same side as John Toshack, who joined Cardiff City and is now with Liverpool. Terry didn't go to Ninian Park, though, because a Leeds scout spotted him, and he was invited up to Elland Road for a look round during the Christmas holidays. At the last minute, the weather caused Terry's trip to be cancelled, and it was Easter time when he finally arrived. He came to stay, and is now a fully-fledged Welsh international.

Terry tells the story of a trial game at Leeds that Easter, when he took a swing at the ball, in the hope of scoring . . . and ended up by falling on his face. Syd Owen was at him straight away to get up and get on with the game. It was Terry's first lesson at Leeds – that you've got to keep right on going. You don't waste time feeling sorry for yourself, or taking a breather.

Terry learned another lesson, about marking men, when he made his debut as a seventeen-year-old against Burnley, and Andy Lochhead, then playing at centre-forward for the Turf Moor club, gave him the slip twice to score goals. There aren't many players who can give Terry the slip these days – he's too quick and alert for that to happen.

He was still only seventeen when he won his first Welsh Under-23 international cap, and he got his full international call-up for Wales against Italy, in Rome – where there was a crowd of 90,000 people. When you have players of the calibre of Terry Yorath around, ready to step in at any time, you are fortunate indeed, and the same can be said about Mick Bates, who did a magnificent job during last season when Johnny Giles was out through injury. Mick himself finished up as a casualty, but it says a lot for him that during his first-team stint, we carried on being unbeaten.

Mick comes from a village near Doncaster, and he was an avid Sheffield Wednesday fan when he was a kid. His grandfathers – yes, both of them – were England schoolboy internationals, and an uncle became a professional footballer, so soccer really ran in the family. Mick played for Doncaster Boys and Yorkshire Boys, and was an England Boys trialist. By that time, four or five clubs had noticed him, and fancied signing him, but Leeds were the club to get him.

Mick reminds me how I invited him to have a game of table-tennis, when he was visiting Elland-road, and says he felt at home straight away, even though he was only a nipper of fifteen. By the time he was sixteen, he was playing in the reserves, and at seventeen he'd made his first-team debut. At twenty-one, he'd played in two Fairs Cup finals, and he's made his mark on quite a few other big-match occasions, since then.

Players such as Terry Yorath and Mick Bates have helped in no small way to keep Leeds United in the forefront. Because we all know that when they're in the team, there won't be a weak link. It's not enough to have a first-class side of 11 players . . . you must have strength in depth, and the men in the squad must be up to the highest standard. Leeds are lucky that they've developed such a strong squad of players, with this one-for-all and all-for-one attitude.

33

# *Shooting Stars -*

## THE GUYS IN THE FRONT LINE

I've scored a few cheeky – and important – goals in my time, such as the ones which took Leeds through a couple of semi-finals to Wembley, and one which put Liverpool out of the Fairs Cup at Anfield. I can still see myself now, facing the Kop and raising both arms in delight, and I kneeled on the ground and grinned my head off. But Billy Bremner isn't really the man on whom Leeds rely for the scoring power – we've got some strikers who know just how to tuck the ball away. And they're internationals, as well as First Division players.

It's often said that the strikers get the glamour treatment, that they hog the headlines. Well, maybe they do – but they certainly take some stick in their opponents' 18-yard box, and one of the bravest fellows I've ever seen is Mick Jones. Just you listen to Allan Clarke talking about Mick, and you'll realise what we all think of this fellow who hails from Worksop, near Nottingham.

They call Allan Clarke 'Sniffer' at Elland Road (me, I'm 'Chalky', on account of my red hair and contrasting complexion), because of his ability to scent out a scoring chance and stick the ball into the back of the net. But 'Sniffer' will tell you himself what a lot of weight Mick Jones takes off his shoulders. Mick is what you might call the straight man of this double act, and he's been worth his weight in gold to Leeds, through the years. It's not just the goals he's scored himself; it's the way he has made it easier for team-mates to snap up the scoring openings. And any centre-half will tell you, too, that when he's been up against Mick, he knows he's been in a game, all right.

Leeds paid Sheffield United £100,000 for the privilege of signing Mick Jones; and he was worth every penny. You just come down to Elland Road, to watch a match, and the odds are that the opposition will be throwing up a defensive wall

*Ready, steady – go! Billy Bremner looks set to slip a pass to a team-mate, as he faces a challenge here.*

at one end of the park. This doesn't make it any easier for our front-line men to get through and score, and it does mean that a striker has to be brave, inside the box. Defenders don't stand on ceremony – and they're usually big lads themselves.

Mick once scored fourteen goals in a schoolboy match, back in Worksop, and that was what gave him the idea that he could shoot a bit! He must have impressed other people, too, for he was picked to play for Worksop Boys and for Nottingham Boys, and when he left school, he went into a side called Dinnington Miners' Welfare. Inside a

*Joe Jordan.*

35

*Mick Jones.*

*Allan Clarke.*

*Peter Lorimer.*

*Eddie Gray.*

(Above): *Surrounded – well almost! That's the Wolves 'keeper, as he clutches the ball, with Billy Bremner (No. 4) and Mick Jones alert for the slightest slip on the goalie's part.*
(Below): *Hey, mind my back! And this is a real tangle in the Manchester United penalty area, as Mick Jones and Gordon McQueen get airborne, seeking to beat United centre-half Jim Holton.*

*My ball! And there's determination written all over the face of Mick Jones, as he is challenged by John McAlle, of Wolves.*

*Heads I win! Allan Clarke, wearing the colours of England, goes up despite the challenge of Manchester United's Scotland forward, Lou Macari. And watching, just in case he gets a break, is England's Peter Storey.*

year, Sheffield United were on his trail. Like other aspiring professionals before him, Mick learned every aspect of his trade – such as sweeping the stands and cleaning the boots of the first-team players – at Bramall Lane.

But just before his eighteenth birthday, he got his big reward – a place in the League side, against Manchester United at Old Trafford. His first League goal came four days later, when he played on his eighteenth birthday against Manchester City, and he scored twice in that game. He's been scoring ever since, too, for now he's hit more than a century of goals, in League games and Cup-ties. One of them won the Fairs Cup for Leeds, a few seasons ago, because it was the only one scored in the two-legged final against Ferencvaros, the Hungarian side.

Oddly enough, the two Micks at Elland Road come from footballing families, for you will remember that I told you Mick Bates's grandfathers and one of his uncles played football; well,

Mick Jones's Dad was a goalkeeper with Worksop Town. And talking of football running in families brings me to Allan Clarke, who is one of three brothers to make the grade in League football. The others are Frank Clarke, now with Carlisle, after a spell at Ipswich Town, and Derek Clarke, who plays for Oxford United. In addition, there are younger brothers Kelvin (he's with Walsall) and Wayne – forwards again, like the other three – and Allan's Dad was a forward who played part-time football with Bangor City.

Allan Clarke and I have one thing in common – we both thought a tremendous lot of Johnny Haynes, who played for Fulham and England. 'Sniffer' grew up in the game alongside Johnny, and I used to idolise this fellow, who could pass a ball so precisely. It's nothing less than the truth, when I admit that if there's one player I've tried to model my game on, so far as the art of passing

*C-o-n-g-r-a-t-u-l-a-t-i-o-n-s! And you can see the joy on the faces of these England players, after a goal has been scored. Can you put a name to the faces? – Left to right, it's Mick Channon, Alan Ball (No. 7), Colin Bell (background), Allan Clarke, Martin Peters and Emlyn Hughes.*

40

*Marching orders from referee Malcolm Sinclair? – No . . . Allan Clarke isn't in trouble. He's just getting a breather, as Mr. Sinclair points to signal the award of a free-kick.*

a ball is concerned, that player was Johnny Haynes. They used to say that Johnny could appear petulant during a game, if something had gone wrong – well, he was usually registering annoyance with himself, if a pass hadn't been absolutely inch-perfect. And I've been known to scowl now and again, myself, when I've tried something and it hasn't come off.

But let's get back to Allan Clarke, who cost Leeds a record fee at the time of £165,000, when he was signed from

Leicester City. I'll admit that I wondered a little bit what he would be like, as a team-mate. Oh, I'd played against him, and knew what he could do; but he had a bit of a reputation for being a player who kept himself to himself. But he soon let us all see that if we were prepared to accept him as one of us, then he was more than willing to go half-way and become a team-mate in every sense of the word.

Allan had been with two or three clubs before he arrived at Elland Road,

41

and he has admitted since that he was really amazed by the family spirit that existed at Leeds. Not that his other clubs were bad ones, or anything like that . . . it was just that he had never imagined how close a bunch of players and their manager, and the rest of the backroom staff, could become. Now, of course, he accepts it all as part of the Leeds United scene. But I know he realises, as we all do, that a lot of hard work went into making Leeds the sort of club it was when he joined us, and the sort of club it remains today. It isn't often that lads who come to Elland Road ask away, and when they do, it's because they have waited so long to nail down a first-team place, and finally decide – even then, reluctantly – that the only way to become a regular in the top flight is to try a change of club.

Allan Clarke and Mick Jones have worked up a tremendous partnership, and it brings each player his share of the goals. Mick, as I've said, is the straight man of the double act – he's direct, and he goes in for the kill. 'Sniffer' goes in for the kill, too – and he's deadly in execution – but he doesn't always advertise the fact that he's around to spell danger.

When he joined Leeds United, manager Don Revie made it clear that at Elland Road we really played a team game – then he told 'Sniffer' to go out and play his natural game. And Allan Clarke's natural game is one in which he is the hunter . . . with the ball as his ammunition, and the target the goal. He can stick them in with his feet or his head, and some of the goals he's scored have surprised even me. It just hasn't seemed on, and 'Sniffer' has been in anything but an ideal position for a scoring attempt – then, suddenly, you'll realise he was lurking in space, and stuck the ball past the 'keeper.

With Mick Jones, you never get the chance to forget that he's around; with 'Sniffer' Clarke, you forget him at your peril . . . and he is so crafty in his movements, at times, that he's gone 'missing' – until he pops up to launch himself at the ball and head it home, or swivel and whip in a shot which is in the net before you've realised it. I like to think that we've all helped Allan Clarke do his job better, and he has said more than once that he wished he'd landed at Leeds earlier than he did, because he believes he would have been an even better player. That I doubt; although I think it's possible that he would have become as accomplished as he is now a little sooner.

Any way, 'Sniffer' started out in football by playing for his home-town club, Walsall, and in those days he was pint-sized. There isn't too much of him today, so far as brawn goes, but he tells us that he really was a little tich. When he left school he didn't stand four feet six inches tall. But he was scoring goals, all the same, and after playing for South-East Staffordshire Boys, he went on the ground staff at Walsall, and signed professional two years later, when he was seventeen. At the end of his first full season in League football, he'd slotted home 23 goals – and he was still only seventeen. By the time he was

*Joe Jordan.*

eighteen, he had moved south, to Fulham, and it was there, of course, that he came under the influence of Johnny Haynes. Johnny and George Cohen, who won a World Cup medal as England's right-back in the 1966 final at Wembley, did a great deal to help young Allan Clarke, and he isn't too proud to tell you that today. George used to go round to see 'Sniffer' on a Sunday morning, and talk football with him, pointing out the things he'd done well, and where he'd gone wrong, in the match the previous day, and Allan took

it all in. He had the sense to realise that you could always learn from a fellow-professional, especially someone who was as accomplished a defender as George Cohen.

So Allan learned as he went along – and he kept on scoring those goals. He did his job so well that Leicester came along, and persuaded Fulham to let him go to Filbert Street, and it was there that he played in his first F.A. Cup final, and won the Player of the Match award, though his side was defeated by that other City, Manchester. Exactly one

43

*It's all action, as Eddie Gray concentrates on the play.*

year after he had gone to Wembley with Leicester, 'Sniffer' was walking out on to Wembley turf again, this time with Leeds United, for the 1970 final against Chelsea.

It was another final which was to end in disappointment for us all, just like the first time when Leeds had gone to Wembley and been beaten in extra time by Liverpool, in 1965. That day, I really thought I'd put us back in the game when I scored, but Ian St. John came up with the winner in extra time. Against Chelsea, we scored twice – through Jack Charlton and Mick Jones – but Peter Houseman and Ian Hutchinson replied for our opponents, and the game finished with the scoreline still reading 2–2, after extra time.

In the replay, at Old Trafford, Mick Jones was on target again, but Peter Osgood and David Webb saw Chelsea home and dry, and they carried the Cup off in triumph back to London. 'Sniffer' Clarke made his third F.A. Cup-final appearance in four years, when he went to Wembley again with Leeds, against Arsenal in 1972, and this time he gained a deserved reward. Not only did he collect that elusive winner's medal . . . he scored the goal that took the F.A. Cup to Leeds. He was there again last year, too, only this time the boot was on the other foot, for the only goal of that final came from our opponents, Sunderland, and Ian Porterfield was the man who scored it. But Allan Clarke could so easily have been a hero for us again, because he had cruel luck with more than one effort. Still, it's not the near-misses that count, is it?

Now you've got a pretty good idea about the sort of partnership Mick Jones and Allan Clarke have struck up, at Leeds. But, of course, there are a few other characters who can get goals, as well. I won't say I've saved the best until the last, because it wouldn't be true . . . but I've saved the Scots until the last . . . and they've played their part in our success, over the years. So if you want to know all about Messrs. Lorimer, Gray and Jordan, internationals all, read on . . .

# Members

# of

# 'The Clan'

You won't find any cliques at Leeds United, but it is a fact that Scots have a tendency to band together and proclaim the virtues of our own brand of football. We like to think that Scotland has given some very talented footballers to the game south of the Border, and a glance around the playing staffs of most top clubs in England will confirm this. Certainly, Leeds United have recruited their share of players from Scotland, and I don't think we have let the club down. Three of the Scots who form part of the Elland Road 'clan' are forwards – Eddie Gray, Peter Lorimer and Joe Jordan. Eddie comes from Glasgow, Peter from Angus and Joe from Carluke.

Peter Lorimer, in fact, set a record the first time he played for our first team, because, at fifteen, he became the youngest player ever to appear in Leeds United's League side. He had played just eight games in the reserves, when he was pitched into the first team, because

we were having injury problems and, like me, when I made my bow against Chelsea, he was out on the wing. The ferocity of Peter Lorimer's shooting – we call him 'Lash', for obvious reasons – is well enough known, by now, but he was whacking home the goals as a kid, before anyone had heard his name. As a schoolboy footballer, he scored close on 200 goals, and it wasn't surprising that such a sharp-shooter should get into Scotland's schoolboy international side. Not surprising, either, that professional clubs should start taking an interest . . . including, of course, Leeds United.

So Peter joined the 'clan' at Elland Road, and it was there that he broke into English League football as a fifteen-year-old. Leeds had been keeping an eye on him since the days when he was playing for a schools team in Dundee, and they didn't forget him, as sometimes happens with youngsters who are living

No time for the clever stuff here – Manchester United defender Martin Buchan tries to whip the ball clear, despite being surrounded by Leeds United opponents.

This is a Lorimer 'special' – though the Leeds man isn't even in the picture – and it takes Wolves 'keeper Phil Parkes all his time (and some acrobatics) to turn the shot round the post.

many miles away from a club. In fact, when manager Don Revie drove up to sign Peter, he got 'booked' ... for speeding! I think 'the Boss' had got a whiff that someone else was on the trail, and he didn't want to be pipped at the post, so he drove up to Scotland as quickly as possible, got Peter's signature on the form that mattered, and was driving back to Leeds in the early hours of the following morning.

'Lash' loves scoring goals – and he's hit some beauties in his time. He still recalls, with tremendous satisfaction, knocking in a hat-trick when we played Bury in an F.A. Cup-tie, and I can tell you that when he lets fly, the goalkeeper is like a cat on hot bricks, because the power of the shot is so great.

Like Terry Cooper, Peter Lorimer has known the hard grind of regaining fitness, after a broken leg – it happened when 'Lash' was still a member of Leeds United's youth team, and we played an F.A. Youth Cup-tie against Sheffield United. Peter, who had three or four first-team outings behind him, was looking set for stardom when he broke a leg in that tie. He was seventeen and for a short time, he worried and wondered if his career was going to be over almost before it had started.

Once he had got the plaster off his leg, it was a hard slog back to fitness, and it meant going back to square one, too, for 'Lash' had to work his way up again through the junior and reserve sides. It took five months before he was ready to stake a claim for a first-team place again. So you will realise, when you think of Peter, and Terry Cooper, that

soccer isn't all glamour, even if you become an international. It hasn't been all glamour for Eddie Gray, either, even if he did win the Man of the Match award when we played Chelsea in the F.A. Cup final at Wembley. Eddie has had more than his fair share of injuries, and last season again, he was out of action for a lengthy spell.

Like Peter Lorimer, Eddie won Scottish international honours as a youngster – he played for Glasgow Boys, and for Scotland Schoolboys – and he had the chance to go to Glasgow Celtic. His Dad wouldn't have argued about that, either, for he was Celtic daft, but Eddie went down to have a look at the Leeds United set-up, and he decided that Elland Road was the place for him.

You know, when you see the players trot out on the park on a Saturday afternoon, in their immaculate white strip, they look like superbly trained and superbly fit athletes – which, of course, they are. But what you don't see, often enough, is the sheer graft that sometimes goes into getting an injured player fit to take his place in the line-up on a Saturday. Eddie Gray, like Terry Cooper and Peter Lorimer, knows all about that side, the unglamorous side, of the game.

He hadn't been with us long when he injured a thigh muscle, and it took a long time to get fit again. It's when you see the rest of the lads taking part in five-a-sides and full-scale, all-out training sessions, that you tend to become discouraged, if you're the one who's having to do a bit of light jogging on your own, or grind away at exercises.

*It looks like ballet on the Soccer field . . . but it's Joe Jordan (Leeds) taking on the Arsenal defence.*

And that thigh injury had the backroom boys at Leeds working overtime on Eddie Gray, day after day, week after week, until in the end, the damage had been repaired and he was ready for a game once more.

It was a difficult time for Eddie last season, too, especially when he could see how Scotland were making their way to the World Cup finals, and he was out of action at Leeds. But he had company, for apart from Terry Copper, who finally made it back, there were other players out of action for lengthy spells through injury. Johnny Giles and Mick Bates were two of them, and Johnny's injury was just about the worst he had ever had during his career in football. He was fighting to regain fitness for about four months, and that's a long time to take out of a playing season.

It's when injuries strike that the real strength of a club becomes apparent, and Leeds, fortunately, were able to take the blows virtually in their stride, for

49

there was always someone ready to step into the breach. And one Scot who did a very efficient job in this direction was Joe Jordan.

At varying times, we were without the services of Allan Clarke and Mick Jones, so Joe got a considerable number of first-team games behind him, and with every match he played, he improved his all-round game. Joe knew, when he came to Elland Road, that it might well be a case of waiting in the wings for a considerable time, before he could stake a claim to a regular first-team place, for with strikers of the calibre of 'Sniffer' Clarke and Mick Jones, you've got to wait for injuries to crop up before you're called into action.

Joe had played quite a few games for us, in the previous couple of seasons, and he did well enough to nail down a place in Scotland's World Cup team. I think the way he has come on, and the fact that we're undoubtedly going to hear a lot more of him, during the next few years, is a tribute both to the work the backroom staff have done on Joe, and to the judgment of a fellow who used to play for Leeds United and Everton – Bobby Collins. For it was Bobby, a former Scotland international, who recommended Joe Jordan to Leeds. I told you we Scots stick together, didn't I?

Bobby did a great job for Leeds when he joined us from Everton. When the

*Down they go! Arsenal 'keeper Bob Wilson and a defender are floored, as Joe Jordan (Leeds) makes no mistake with this ground shot.*

*Tea up! And taking a welcome break are (left to right) Leeds players Mick Bates, Eddie Gray, Terry Yorath and Gordon McQueen.*

time came for him to move on, he went to Bury, and then back north of the Border, to play for Morton. And it was there that he saw young Joe, and realised the potential he had. Bobby didn't take long to weigh up what Joe Jordan could do, given the chance to join a crack club like Leeds, and he contacted manager Don Revie to say: 'I've seen a lad who can make the grade at the top – he's worth spending a bit of money on.'

Leeds did spend a bit of money, too – something like £15,000 – and they signed a future Scotland international, on the strength of Bobby Collins' recommendation. Joe is firmly established now as a member of the first-team squad at Elland Road, and I'm certain that he will become a big name and a big favourite with our fans, as the seasons go by. He's strong, he's brave, he's direct. He can hit a ball and he can head a ball – and defenders know he's around.

Yes, our Scottish 'clan' has certainly grown, since the days when I travelled south of the Border with my pal, Tommy Henderson, and we threw in our lot with Leeds. But the family spirit hasn't changed a bit, in all the time I've been at Elland Road.

51

Talk to big Jack Charlton, who is now the manager of Middlesbrough, and he'll tell you about the bingo sessions before the games; talk to other players still on the staff, and they'll tell you how our manager had his little superstitions – such as wearing the same blue suit on match days, until it became almost threadbare. We've laughed a lot, as well as suffered a few heartaches, and we've kept on going, shrugging off failure and looking for success again the following season.

In the early days, some folk thought we played it a bit too hard, a bit too tough; but we at Leeds believe that last season, we finally nailed the criticisms. We've won over a lot of people with our brand of football, our readiness to entertain and make a game of it. We've tried to bring a bit of showbiz into the game, with our greetings to the fans before the kick-off, and our distinctive track suits and strip. Above all, we've gone out to play the kind of football which not only wins matches, but wins the fans – even if they're not Leeds United supporters. The tributes we received, and the gates we commanded, last season, proved a point, I reckon.

Leeds United have a growing following, these days; there are youngsters (and a few elderly folk) all round the country who stick up for Leeds United. And it must be because they have felt that we had something to offer which they appreciated and enjoyed. That can't be bad, now, can it?

I hope, now that I've introduced you to the lads who are my team-mates, now that I've taken you behind the scenes a bit at Elland Road and shown you what sort of manager, what sort of backroom staff, what sort of players we have, that you feel you've really come to know us. And I hope that the next time you see us go out on the park, and raise our arms in a friendly salute, you'll give us a wave back.

Later in this book, I'll be saying a word or two about the World Cup, and about Scotland. Right now, there are plenty of other stories for you to read ... stories by some of the big-name players from other clubs. I'll admit that when we meet on the field, we don't ask for or give any quarter; but off the field, we can be good pals. And I'm sure you'll enjoy reading what they have to say, about themselves, their clubs, and about the game in general.

# Exciting? – That's Alan Hudson!

## says GORDON BANKS

I've known some truly great footballers in my time; but I can honestly say there is no one who has excited me more than one of the young stars at Stoke City, my own club. And his name is Alan Hudson.

In my playing career, I collected seventy-three caps for England, and apart from the games I played for my first club, Chesterfield, and my second club, Leicester City, I clocked up 246 competitive matches for Stoke. I played in two World Cup tournaments, and against some of the world's crack footballing teams, and in the process, I came to recognise many formidable opponents at close quarters. I don't think anyone would argue against the claim that I reckon by now to be able to spot a class footballer when I see one. And Alan Hudson, Stoke's £240,000 signing from Chelsea, very definitely comes into that category.

I'm a bit past the stage of hero-worship now, although when I was a young-

*Gordon Banks.*

ster back in Sheffield, and kicking a ball around at every possible opportunity, my idol in those days was Manchester City's German-born goalkeeper, Bert Trautmann. We didn't have a television in our house, and I didn't get to many matches, because I was so busy playing

53

myself; but I did used to make sure I went to my pals' homes when there was a match on telly . . . and I was delighted whenever I saw Bert in action. In fact, I was enthralled. He was so brave, so agile, so skilled and had such uncanny reflex actions . . . he had the lot.

Then I became a professional footballer myself, and as time went by, I made the grade at international level. I played in the 1966 World Cup, and collected a winner's medal with England there, and I decided that Uwe Seeler, the West German striker, was one of the really great players, too. As time went on, and Franz Beckenbauer gained in experience and reputation, I added him to my list . . . and Gerd Mueller, who followed Seeler as a scoring ace for West Germany.

After that, I learned to appreciate what a tremendous midfield player Gunter Netzer had become, when he was with Borussia Moenchengladbach – and, of course, as an international with West Germany. And I added to my list again when I saw the Dutch ace, Johann Cruyff, in action for Ajax. Netzer went to Real Madrid, and Cruyff went to Barcelona, and that in itself proved what these players were worth.

You may be surprised that I haven't yet mentioned the one and only Edson Arantes Nascimento – Pele, to you – but I'm coming to him now. He was the greatest all-round player I ever came up against, and I know from first-hand experience what a danger-man he could be. People still stop me and ask me to tell them all about that save I made from Pele in the 1970 World Cup in Brazil.

They also ask me about Eusebio, the star striker with the Eagles of Lisbon, Benfica, and again I have to say that this fellow, so modest and unassuming off the field, yet such a deadly marksman on it, figures in my personal list of greats. There are others, of course, and they are English players – Bobby Charlton, a great friend of mine, figures high on the list. And from Italy, there is Dino Zoff, the goalkeeper. I reckon that by now I know a good deal about the requirements for my own position, and Zoff became my No. 1 'keeper last year, when I watched him in action.

So you see I have built up a list of around ten or a dozen players who will live for ever in my memory. And this brings me to Alan Hudson, still only twenty-three, and destined to become one of the best footballers we have seen in these islands for a long, long time. My memory of Alan is still of the day he made his debut for Stoke – and it was under exceptionally trying circumstances.

It wasn't so much that he had been in dispute with his club, Chelsea, or even the fact that he had cost Stoke their biggest-ever fee of £240,000. It was the fact that he had so much to live up to, on his debut day – because apart from that fee, Stoke were playing Liverpool, and Alan knew that there would be a bumper crowd for Stoke, with every eye watching his every move. And against a team of the calibre of Liverpool, who were the League champions and U.E.F.A. Cup holders, it really was a test of your own ability and character.

Normally, Stoke's home gate for a League game had been around 18,000, up to Alan's debut last season. On that day, the gate topped 31,000. And believe me, with Liverpool still grimly chasing Leeds United, who were hot-footing it for the title, we all knew that Bill Shankly's men would give absolutely nothing away. More than that – they would be trying to make sure that they kept Alan Hudson quiet.

Alan had been at Stoke only a few days, so he hadn't had much time to get to know his new team-mates, although he had been staying with my old World Cup buddy, Geoff Hurst. But Alan hadn't played a First Division game for three weeks, and I suspected that the pace of this one would tell on him after a bit. I also wondered if nerves would play havoc with his form. I needn't have worried . . .

In the dressing-room before the match, there were cards and telegrams of good wishes for him. As I know from experience again, these can be a boost to you . . . and they can have the effect of making you even more keyed up. Alan admitted that he was nervous, knowing that all the fans were going to be keeping a close eye on his every move. It wasn't just Liverpool who would be 'marking' him! But the moment he got his first touch of the ball, he showed that he had the character and the ability to overcome nerves.

The Stoke lads soon got him involved, and for his part, he showed straight away that he wasn't going to hide. He wanted the ball, and when he got it, he used it to great effect. He master-minded the midfield for Stoke, he got in two or three good shots, and he really took charge. Even Bill Shankly was moved to say, after the match, that he had done well and should do even better, when he had settled in – and Bill doesn't shout the praises of the opposition as a rule! Peter Dobing, Stoke's former skipper, was at the game, and he weighed in with his share of praise, as well. 'Fantastic!' was Peter's assessment. And he knows what midfield play is all about.

Peter had had to hang up his boots because of a back injury, but he was full of admiration for Alan Hudson that day. As for manager Tony Waddington, as he explained afterwards: 'It took Gordon Banks a few months to win over the Potteries fans, who don't give their affections easily, and it took Jimmy Greenhoff about a year to do it. This lad (Alan Hudson) had them eating out of his hand in about three minutes flat, this afternoon. I don't need to say anything about his performance . . . he let his feet do the talking for him, on the field of play.'

I watched Alan closely in training, after that game, and in other matches that he played. And I came to realise that his debut performance hadn't been a flash in the pan. He's taller than you would imagine, when you see him at a distance on the park; stand close up to him, and you realise he's not too far off the six-foot mark. And although he's slimly built, he's far from being a frail figure – he can shield the ball, and takes some knocking off it when he does so. He can ride a tackle, and he can win the ball, too, and he can beat a man by dribbling, and by bending a pass round him.

A few years ago, England's former team manager, Sir Alf Ramsey, described Martin Peters as 'ten years ahead of his time'. I think it was also Sir Alf who described Alan Hudson as the most exciting young player to come on the scene for years. Alan collected England Under-23 honours, but got himself into a bit of bother when he cried off an England Under-23 tour – he and Derby County's Colin Todd were banned from international football for two years. The ban was later lifted, and I know that when Alan came to Stoke, he was determined to play his way back into international favour.

In the past, it's always been a case of players moving to London to make a name for themselves. The big London clubs have been regarded as the ones where you are noticed. Alan Hudson was with a big London club, and he had been noticed, but – and I know he won't mind me saying so – he had blotted his copy-book. He decided, when he was in dispute with Chelsea, that his career as a footballer had come to the crossroads – and I think he chose a very brave course. I also believe he made a very wise decision, to reverse the trend, and leave the big city for the Potteries. He knew he had to get his career sorted out, and he made the break.

That, in itself, took quite a bit of courage, for he and his wife were used to London – it was their home, and they didn't know Stoke well at all, apart from the fact that once a season, Chelsea used to play at the Victoria Ground in the League.

The signing itself had a cloak-and-dagger touch about it, because our manager, Tony Waddington, dashed down to London and left the team, who were travelling on to Ipswich for a League match the following day. Tony had arranged to contact Alan at an hotel, but when he reached the hotel, he discovered that another team was staying there overnight, and he nipped into a phone box, to avoid being recognised. At that stage, no one knew that Stoke had agreed terms with Chelsea – and even Alan Hudson didn't know which club he was being asked to join. He and Tony Waddington made the rendezvous in a London park, and it wasn't long before Alan decided to make the break and move to the Potteries.

He has been with us for only a few months, even now, but I am convinced that we have made one of the greatest signings for many years. I am also convinced that Alan Hudson, who came to Stoke because he was a man with a mission, will accomplish that mission successfully before he has finished. Stoke haven't been noted for being the most fashionable club in the country, although we have had a few international players on our books, such as Geoff Hurst and George Eastham, but I believe that Alan Hudson made up his mind that Stoke were shortly going to have another England man on their staff – himself.

It is my honest opinion that moving to Stoke was the best thing Alan could have done. He's made a new start to his career – and he's still got ten years ahead of him in top-class football. I am certain that he can nail down a regular place in

England's side, and that he can fulfil all the promise he displayed in his early days as a first-teamer at Chelsea. Greatness is a label which has to be earned, and Alan Hudson has shown he wants to earn not just the reward of England honours, but the tag of being regarded as a great footballer. From what I have seen, he will succeed in his mission.

# Mike Channon –
## 'A Professional's Professional'

He stands six feet tall, weighs in at 12 stone 7 pounds . . . and there is no doubt that for every pound he weighs, he would be worth many more pounds in hard cash. He is the striker every manager in the country would love to sign . . . but he belongs to Southampton. And, of course, his name is Mike Channon.

Ten years have gone by since Wiltshire-born Mike signed for the Saints, as they are known, when he left his schooldays behind him. His name was unknown in professional football then; but in the past few seasons, he has made his mark all right – usually with a goal or two. For that's how opposing defenders remember the impact Mike Channon has made on a game.

England had just won the World Cup, and we were basking in the reflected glory of this triumph, back in 1966, when Mike Channon made his debut for Southampton in League football.

Four years after that, he was being talked about as 'a highly rated young forward'. The Soccer reference books didn't give him more than three or four lines of space, though – where Jack Charlton merited nine lines, Channon's career to date was summed up with the recording of his birthplace (Orcheston, Wilts.), his club and the date he joined the Saints. There were no England Under-23 honours after his name, never mind full international appearances.

By and by, though, one defender after another was saying to himself: 'This lad's good – he's dangerous in the air and on the ground. He takes some watching, and he takes some stopping. And I'll certainly be on my guard against him next time we meet.'

For Mike Channon, having established himself in the Southampton team, was beginning to give defenders a hard time. And he was one of the major factors in deciding – perhaps indirectly –

*Mick Channon, of Southampton and England, in full stride – and trying to find a way through the Poland defence.*

*Hands off! Left to right, Allan Clarke, Mick Channon – both of England – and Billy Bremner's Scotland international team-mate, Danny McGrain.*

the future of Martin Chivers, who had already proved himself a prolific goal-scorer with the Saints. By 1968, Southampton were satisfied that in Channon, they had a striker who could fill Chivers' boots and follow in his scoring footsteps – so they could afford to sell Chivers to Tottenham for £125,000.

Channon proved that he could be direct, as a striker; that he could hit a ball hard, and that he could use his head to nod the ball home. And the bigger clubs began following him around . . . but to no purpose. Southampton were adamant that he was simply not for sale – even at £300,000.

Chivers had gone, but the Saints had a new striking partnership of Channon and Welsh international Ron Davies. Between them, they carved up opposing defences, and scored goals. And although Davies finally moved on, to Portsmouth, Channon remained at The Dell – and he kept on sticking the ball into the net. By the start of the 1973–74 season, he had really hit the big-time, collected several Under-23 caps, and forced his way into the full England side. He had also played 229 League games for the Saints, and scored seventy nine goals.

One man who has seen the development of Mike Channon since the first day he arrived at Southampton is Terry Paine, himself a player of vast ability and experience. Terry is Southampton's longest-serving player, with no fewer than eighteen seasons of football behind him, and he has seen it all, in his time. He has been through the Third and Second Division to the First, with Southampton, gained nineteen full England caps and a dozen other representative honours, and was in England's World Cup-winning squad in 1966.

Terry, who signed professional for the Saints back in 1957, made his Football League debut on his eighteenth birthday, became a first-team regular and club captain, and last season chalked up his 800th appearance for Southampton in League and Cup matches. This ever-green player was once regarded as an out-and-out winger, but in recent seasons he has switched to a midfield role, and from there he has been able to assess the striking ability of Channon, as well as provide the service for Mike to get many of his goals.

The Terry Paine verdict on his England team-mate: 'He is one of the most professional professionals I've ever played alongside. And I've seen his progress right the way through, since he arrived as a youngster aged about fifteen. In many ways, one game against Tottenham in season 1972–73 summed up all that is best in Mick – he absolutely ran them ragged that day. Not everything he tried came off, but we beat them in the end, and it was mainly due to him. I think he scored a couple of goals himself, but the feature of his game was the running he did, the way he worked to make things work for his team-mates. Of all the games I have seen Mick play, I still rate that one as a tremendous performance.

'There have been other occasions, too – I can recall an F.A. Cup replay at Old Trafford, when we lost in extra time; there was a game against Leeds, when he started moving around the half-way line, took on Norman Hunter, won the duel, and pushed the ball past the 'keeper; there was a Cup-tie against Newport, when we were drawing 2–2, and Mick hammered the ball home from the edge of the 18-yard box, to give us the winner. The ball fairly flew into the far corner of the net. And there was a diving header, when we were playing Newcastle United. Mick threw himself full length at the ball, and he headed it beyond the Newcastle defence.

'Believe me, it's a pleasure playing with Mick Channon. He's a very exciting player, particularly impressive when the going is good. He's a big fellow, of course, and when the ground is exceptionally heavy, it means he can't take off on those runs quite the same ... but when he gets going in full flight, there's no one in the country who can stop him. If he has a weakness – and I think he would admit this himself – it is that sometimes he doesn't finish as well as he might, in the sense that now and again, he'll try to make too sure, instead of letting fly first time. But, having said that, the figures show that he's still scored a heck of a lot of goals.

'Undoubtedly, his greatest asset is his running off the ball, and his ability to take people on. He's a lot more skill than some folk might think – he's got tremendous acceleration, and when he's in full stride, no one can touch him. He doesn't just go through for the ball to come to his feet; he does the hardest thing in the game, by running off the ball and into space. I've not seen his like since Jimmy Greaves was making us marvel at his ability to get into scoring positions.

'If midfield players had more men like Mick Channon to play with, it would make their job a great deal easier. He's great for a midfield man, such as myself, because he gets into so many scoring positions, and I know that when I knock the ball into space, Mick will appear and take it from there.'

So much for an assessment of Mick Channon from an experienced international who is also a Southampton team-mate. Terry Paine might be considered to be biased in favour of Channon ... although few would even attempt to argue this. But, just in case, let's see what another one-time international has to say about the strapping Southampton striker. Come in, Keith Newton, Burnley and England international left-back, who has played in the World Cup and knows the merits of opposing strikers at top level.

Newton says about Channon: 'He's brilliant, at times. He can go on his own. And he isn't all brute force, even if he is strong runner – there's plenty of skill packed into that frame of his. For me, Mick Channon is an all-round player. He has ability in the air, he knows how to shoot, he knows how to take a man on, and he has a good turn of speed. When you've said all that, you've summed up virtually the complete footballer – and I can't pay Mick Channon any greater tribute than that.'

Newton himself is no slouch, as a defender and as a footballer. He gained recognition at England level when he was playing for Blackburn Rovers, moved to Everton for an £80,000 fee, and was there for the run-in to the First Division championship. Burnley snapped him up when Everton let him go on a free transfer, and he's since been showing he can more than hold his own in the top flight. Keith Newton knows a worthy opponent, when he sees one . . and clearly he gives Channon top marks as a striker.

Apart from his England caps, Channon has seen only one honour come Southampton's way ... when they gained promotion from the Second Division, with Manchester City, in 1966. And he was just starting his career then. But last year, he signed a lucrative contract which tied him to the Saints for the foreseeable future. Shortly afterwards, he was quizzed about playing for a club which had a crowd capacity of only 30,000 – and an average gate of something like 18,000. He gave a straightforward answer: 'You can't expect to get honour and glory by chasing about from club to club.'

Channon talked about sorting out 'your own priorities in life', and admitted that he thoroughly enjoyed being down at Southampton, for it meant that he could live in the countryside, which 'means so much to me'. He had just moved into a farmhouse which had a 'spread' of four acres. He did admit that circumstances can change – and there are plenty of big clubs who would like nothing better than to change the circumstances for Mike Channon – but it seems that Southampton get some sort of a hold on the players they discover.

Ron Davies was there for a lengthy spell. Terry Paine – once ambitious to get to a First Division club – was persuaded to stay, and he finally made it with the Saints; Hughie Fisher and Brian O'Neil have been at The Dell a fair time; John McGrath remained as a coach, when he hung up his playing boots; and Mick Channon has been there for a decade now. He could well complete his career as a one-club man, too, for now that he's broken through to the full England side, he knows that honours at international level don't depend upon your being with one of the so-called glamour clubs. And as for Southampton, Lawrie McMenemy, who succeeded Ted Bates as team manager, has already shown that he has a flair for success. The Saints may have gone down to Division 2, but Mick Channon is confident they'll climb back. And he'll still be in their ranks, when they do.

# The
# BALL GAME

## by JOHN ADAMS

Ever since football – or soccer, as it is more widely known throughout the world – began, there have been changes. Certainly, so far as this country is concerned, some of the earliest knowledge of the game being played in a rough form relates to the Roman soldiers ... the conquerors who played the game as they forced their way up the country, building the roads which are still the backbone of our communications system.

Obviously, they did not have any of the sophisticated equipment we use today; but they did still play a form of the game, And even now, one can see the game being played in various forms, and with various types of equipment.

When I was a boy, the Hungarians had just defeated England for the first time in an international played in this country, and the star of that team was Ferenc Puskas – 'the galloping major', as he became known. For as well as

being a star footballer, he was in the Army. Like many youngsters who were captivated by the Hungarians' perform-ance, and especially that of Puskas, I made it my business to find out some-thing about his life story.

He related how he was born into a family in Budapest which could not afford luxuries – even a proper football was beyond his means – and so he developed his skill, as he went on errands, by dribbling a 'ball' made out of rags wrapped together. And today you'll still see youngsters 'making do' as they practice in the school play-ground or on spare land. Often enough, the ball is a tennis ball; but modern technical advances have brought the plastic football much more on to the scene.

When I was a youngster, I was a pretty popular character around Christ-mas time – because each year my present was a new, leather football. And at that time, we all looked upon this as the only 'proper' football . . . in fact, it was unthinkable that the game at top level could ever be played with anything other than a leather football.

There were times, when Christmas was due, and I was awaiting impatiently the replacement of the leather ball that was coming apart at the seams, when we had to make do with 'inferior' footballs. I can even remember playing soccer in the school yard with a stone. It may have helped to improve my dribbling skill, but it did little to inspire my enthusiasm for the game when someone gave the stone a heart kick and it rapped me on the ankle!

Nowadays, youngsters can think themselves luckier, because the cheaply-produced plastic footballs are available and easily replaced. And if you think that this is still only an inferior substitute for the real thing, I've got news for you . . . because it is possible, almost a certainty, that international matches will soon be played with footballs made of a material other than leather.

In the past year or so, you've all heard and read about world shortages of this and that; and football manufacturers tell me that there has been increasing difficulty in getting the top-class leather required to make footballs which do not easily lose their shape. Not only that; world prices have been rising – not only for the leather, but for the labour to make the footballs. So before long, the leather ball may be a thing of the past, as old-fashioned as Puskas's rag football or as the type of football the Romans used hundreds of years ago.

But before you begin to worry about the future of the game, or indeed, its very survival, let me add that as one door closes, another always seems to open. And this applies to the game of soccer. In fact, it's possible that already you have played in a game with a football which looked like leather, felt like leather, had all the characteristics of a leather ball . . . but, indeed, wasn't leather.

Think, for a minute, about the shoes on your feet. Only a few years ago, the vast majority of people would not consider wearing anything but leather on their feet – synthetically-manufactured shoes were certainly not all the rage when they came on to the market. But today, the situation is so different – I reckon that just about every person in the country owns at least one pair of shoes that contains little or no leather.

The production of new, synthetic materials has revolutionised the construction of shoes, and it is more than possible that such materials will have a great deal to offer when it comes to manufacturing footballs. As of now, it has been proved that a non-leather football can be produced which is waterproof, hard wearing and which keeps its shape. Such a ball, of course, usually costs considerably more than the average leather ball; but it does have properties which make it an attractive proposition. For one football may last a whole season of matches, where previously two or three leather footballs would have been required during the season. So the initial cost becomes much cheaper, over the long term. So the world shortage of leather doesn't mean the end of the world of soccer!

Which brings me back to the problem of labour, and the cost involved there. Some British manufacturers cut the pieces of leather or synthetic material to shape in this country, drill them with holes for the stitches – then pack the pieces in boxes and send them to faraway spots such as India, Pakistan and even China, where labour costs are so much lower that the job of stitching the footballs together is done for a fraction of the money which would have to be paid out here. When the panels are stitched together, the football is boxed again and transported to this country for the final stages of construction and distribution. And although this may seem a long, involved process, I am assured it is necessary if you are to get a good football which does not cost you too much to buy.

But as living standards are rising around the world, so is the cost of labour in those far-away countries. And, to meet this new problem, manufacturers have come up with new types of material to produce moulded footballs of genuine match quality. The materials involved are not going to be as costly as leather, and that tedious stitching process is eliminated.

Now we have reached a stage where we can get a football for teaching and training, which has excellent properties, and which can be produced for a fraction of the cost of a normal football. And the manufacturers are working on the job of making the football suitable not just for teaching and training, but for match requirements. The ball has to meet the ruling of the game when it comes to weight and circumference, and, of course, the idea is that the football will be exactly the same at the end of the match as it was at the start. Naturally, this type of football is made slightly smaller for youngsters who play in schools' soccer, for instance – and, as I said earlier, you may already have used such a ball in your own school matches.

All through this book, you have been able to read about the star players. But no matter whether it's an international match or a kickabout on the local recreation ground, the teams involved have to play with a football that's suitable for the occasion. Without the ball, there just can't be a game. So it's a comforting thought that, despite the world shortages of this, that and the other, soccer seems to be in no danger of having to fold up. Somehow, I just cannot visualise England playing Brazil at Wembley with a football made out of old rags! And now it looks as if the problem which had cropped up is being solved, for top-class professional soccer, for the schools football enthusiasts and for the kids who form their own teams or play in the back garden just for kicks.

# BOB

# THE

# BOMBSHELL

'I rate him one of the best three centre-forwards in England . . . and I certainly didn't have any sleepless nights about signing a player for £350,000.' The speaker: Everton manager Billy Bingham. And the player to whom he refers: striker Bob Latchford, who became the top-priced player in the country when he joined the Goodison club from Birmingham. Latchford went to Everton in a deal, packaged at £350,000, which also involved the transfer to Birmingham of midfield man Howard Kendall and full-back Arthur Styles.

Billy Bingham says of Latchford: 'It speaks for itself, the fact that so much money was involved – obviously, I thought Bob was worth it, even though it meant letting valuable players leave Everton. But I had no hesitation in signing Bob. He has a great pedigree, so far as scoring goals is concerned. He is a tremendously powerful player in the air, he's physically powerful when it

comes to getting the ball in the 18-yard box – which is essential in modern football – and for a big fellow, he's pretty good on the ground.'

That's a pretty good reference for any manager to give a player. And if you ask Billy Bingham to name the other two strikers who figure in his top trio, it doesn't take him a moment to say: 'Mick Channon, of Southampton, and John Richards, of Wolves.' And he adds: 'I would also put Leeds United's Mick Jones in that category for good measure.'

But back to Bob Latchford . . . who stands six feet tall, tips the scales at 12 stone, is the brother of Birmingham 'keeper Dave Latchford and West Brom 'keeper Peter Latchford . . . and has been known to play in goal himself. That happened last season, when Birmingham's £90,000 signing from Leeds, Welsh international Gary Sprake, was injured on his debut at St. Andrews,

66

against Wolves. The date was October 13, 1973 – but it wasn't unlucky 13 for Latchford, because he didn't concede a goal.

Latchford has become a bit of a specialist in scoring hat-tricks, too. There was a game in the League Cup at Ipswich, when Birmingham were not given much of a chance . . . but Latchford hammered home a magnificent hat-trick, to put paid to Bobby Robson's team – and three days later, he repeated the feat, this time against Leicester City. As if to prove that he had the lot, Latchford scored one goal with his right foot, another with his left, and the third with a header!

Latchford marked his debut for Birmingham by scoring a couple of goals against Preston, in March, 1969. The following season, he was a reserve player once more, after the costly signing of striker Tony Hateley. But soon after Freddie Goodwin became the manager of Birmingham, there was a change in Latchford's fortunes, for he was back in the first team, and catching the limelight along with team-mate Trevor Francis, who himself was making a big name by scoring four goals against Bolton Wanderers in February, 1971 . . . and Francis was then aged only sixteen.

Latchford did his stuff, as well, though, and he finished his first full season in League football with thirteen goals from thirty-five League games. Twice, against Carlisle and Queen's Park Rangers, he was only one goal short of a hat-trick; and the following season, as Birmingham surged through to clinch promotion by a whisker, he

*Bob Latchford.*

was a key man. Five matches went by without him getting even one goal – then he struck, against Charlton, with . . . a hat-trick. Before a month had passed he had done the trick again, this time, against Watford – and then Portsmouth and Swindon felt the impact of his striking power, as he put two goals past each of them.

When the cliffhanger match was

staged, it was against Orient, and Birmingham needed a point to make sure they pipped Millwall for promotion. They won – with a goal from Bob Latchford.

He ended his spell as a Second Division striker with twenty-six League and Cup goals that season, scored on his First Division debut against Sheffield United, and rattled home . . . you've guessed it . . . a hat-trick against Manchester City in the second month of the season. At the end of that first season in the top flight, Bob Latchford had tucked away nineteen scoring chances.

February 15, 1974, was the day Latchford left Birmingham and signed for Everton – and there were plenty of Midland fans who were sorrowful about his departure. They made it clear, too, that they didn't like to lose him; but the deed was done, for Birmingham had decided that the only way to recruit the men they wanted was to let one of their own stars go.

Latchford left Birmingham with an impressive record: he had been the Second Division's leading marksman in season 1971–72, with twenty-three League goals and four F.A. Cup goals; he had been Birmingham's top scorer in season 1972–73 (this was in the First Division, remember), with twenty League and Cup goals. And on the day he joined Everton, he had scored ten goals for Birmingham in the League, five in the Football League Cup, two in the F.A. Cup, and one in the Texaco Cup. In 158 appearances for Birmingham, he had scored sixty-eight goals – almost a goal every other game – and he

had also collected England Under-23 caps against Denmark and against Wales. Indeed, he scored on his first Under-23 outing, against the Danes . . . and it seems that that selection was a timely boost to his confidence, as well as to his career.

For the season of 1973–74 had not been an auspicious one for Bob Latchford. There was a time when, with goals hard to come by, he heard the fans at St. Andrews giving him 'some stick', and he eventually was axed from the first team for a spell, after having scored only three goals in thirteen League games. He admitted that this loss of, striking power had him worried – then Sir Alf Ramsey took a hand, by picking him for the Under-23 game against Denmark. England drew, 1–1, and the goal that Latchford scored was set up by his team-mate from St. Andrews, Trevor Francis, who sent the ball across to him low and hard. Latchford, reading Francis' mind, had embarked on a run which took him into the right position to meet the cross, and he did the rest.

That Under-23 appearance, and that goal, did a great deal to boost Latchford's confidence and restore his belief in himself, and it wasn't long after that he was scoring that hat-trick against Ipswich in the League Cup, and following up three days later with the trio of goals against Leicester.

Bob Latchford, of course, comes from a footballing family, like Leeds United's Allan Clarke. The Clarke brothers are strikers, but Bob Latchford is the odd man out among his brothers, for both Dave and Peter are goalkeepers. In season 1972–73, the Latchfords carved out a bit of football history for themselves, when all three brothers were playing First Division football at the same time. And that must have made their father – who in his Army days played Soccer among professionals – a proud man, indeed.

Bob was spotted by Birmingham chief scout Don Dorman, and he joined the St. Andrews club straight from school. He was powerfully built, in those days, and it wasn't long before the Blues' coaches were taking notice of him. He was in the Birmingham side which reached the final of the F.A. Youth Cup, and graduated to youth-international honours, being capped for England in the 'little World Cup' competition in East Germany in 1969.

When the day came for Birmingham and Bob Latchford to part company, one sportswriter named him 'Bob the Bombshell', and there were plenty of references to the fact that he was joining a club which had been able to boast, at one time, of having the most famed and feared strikers on their books, for William Ralph 'Dixie' Dean and Tommy Lawton became legends in their heydays at Everton.

Many people first realised what an accomplished player Latchford had become, when he went with Birmingham to play against Liverpool at Anfield, in season 1972–73. That afternoon, Liverpool – who were going hard at it for the title, which they did eventually win – found themselves 3–1 down at one stage in the game, and it took a storming rally by Bill Shankly's men to salvage a victory from the jaws of defeat, by finishing up 4–3 winners. Latchford that day was a revelation, wandering out to the wings, taking passes in his stride, and generally creating havoc among the normally composed Liverpool defence. He looked brave, powerful, good in the air and tremendous on the ground. And millions of television viewers were moved to admiration at his non-stop display. Latchford was one of the Birmingham marksmen that afternoon, and even Liverpool supporters admitted as they left the ground after this pulsating feast of football, that he hadn't deserved to finish on the losing side.

Billy Bingham wasn't the manager of Everton at that time, but the Goodison club had already tried their luck for Latchford, without success. In fact, Birmingham chairman Clifford Coombs told the story of how manager Freddie Goodwin had turned a deaf ear to more than one offer made by Everton's then manager, Harry Catterick, and how Everton tried again, after a game between the clubs at Goodison Park, when the Everton chairman at the time, John Moores, suggested that there must be SOME price which Birmingham would accept for their striker. The Coombs answer: 'It's a deal . . . if you offer one of your mail-order businesses and four or five of your stores!'

Of course, at the time it was nonsense to talk in such terms . . . but Everton finally did get their man, when Billy Bingham struck a bargain with Freddie Goodwin. It wasn't quite a mail-order business and four or five stores, but Everton had to part with a full-back, plus one of the best uncapped wing-halves in the country, Howard Kendall, plus £80,000, to land Latchford. And now that he's had a few months to settle down to the way things are worked out at Goodison, they're looking forward to 'Bob the Bombshell' blasting home the goals which will repay that massive outlay in the transfer market. As Billy Bingham says: 'What do I think of Bob Latchford? – that £350,000 transfer deal says it all . . .'

# A Taste of their Own Medicine

## by EMLYN HUGHES

Every player has his favourite position, no matter how versatile he might be. And, if I'm honest, I've got to admit that nothing gives me a bigger kick than going through from midfield, getting to the edge of our opponents' 18-yard box, then cutting inside and having a crack at scoring a goal. I love going forward and giving opposing defences a bit of a grilling, and the fact that I've scored close on half a century of goals for Liverpool must prove something, I feel. Maybe, deep down, I like the feeling that I'm giving the opposition a taste of their own medicine, for as a left-back, I've had plenty of hard graft to do in my time, both with Liverpool and with England.

I started off my football career as a left-back, in fact, – apart from one match, that was where I played all my games for Blackpool. Oddly enough, the one game I played in midfield was against Liverpool, and I was given one of the toughest jobs any player could ever have had . . . for I was told to mark Roger Hunt, the fellow who took the shortest route to goal. It wasn't long after that – I'd played only a couple of dozen matches or so altogether for Blackpool's first team – that I received a phone call from Bloomfield Road, telling me to get down to the ground . . . and there, waiting to sign me, was Liverpool manager Bill Shankly.

I knew all about him and his team, of course, although the closest I had been to getting on the pitch at Anfield was when I went across from Blackpool one night to watch Liverpool playing in a European Cup-tie. I stood in the paddock, that night, and breathed in the tremendous atmosphere which – although I didn't have even an inkling of it, at the time – I was to come to know so well.

71

I can tell you that when Bill Shankly rapped out his question to me, as we stood face to face for the first time, I didn't take more than a few seconds to give him my answer. 'How do you fancy playing for us, son?' he said . . . and his voice seemed to reverberate round the room, as he looked me straight in the eye. It was almost as if he were defying me to even hesitate over my answer. And I signed before he could change his mind!

Three months after having put pen to paper, I was plunged into the first team. A couple of days before Liverpool were due to play against Stoke at Anfield, 'the boss' told me that I would be making my debut – and that I would be playing a midfield role. All I could do was hope that my best would turn out to be good enough. And it seems that I came through the test all right, I've now played something over 400 games for Liverpool, which is not a bad record, I reckon. You won't find my name in the record books, so far as transfer fees go, although the £65,000 Liverpool shelled out for me at the time was a hefty sum to pay for a virtual unknown; but that's the sort of thing Liverpool have made a habit of doing, since I joined them – and who could deny that they have had real value for their money?

Ray Clemence, now an England international goalkeeper, cost Liverpool a mere £18,000 when he was signed from Scunthorpe. Left-back Alec Lindsay – what a left foot this fellow has! – was a £65,000 signing, like myself, only he arrived from Bury. Larry Lloyd cost £50,000, when he joined us from Bristol

*Emlyn Hughes playing for England.*

Rovers – and he's been in the England squad, too. Kevin Keegan was another import from Scunthorpe, and he cost £35,000. What price would he bring today, as a sharp-shooter and a fully-fledged England player? Steve Heighway cost nothing by way of a transfer fee, for he was snapped up from Skelmersdale United, who were then in the Cheshire League and are now in the Northern Premier League, so that was another bargain. And our most recent signings have been a giant young striker named Alan Waddle, who cost £40,000 from Halifax, and midfield player Ian MacDonald, signed for £35,000 from Workington.

It's worth mentioning, too, that Ian and I both hail from Barrow – and that, at one stage in our respective careers, it seemed we would never hit the top, let alone with a crack club like Liverpool. While I was at Blackpool, trying to break through, I had a part-time job, and I felt I wasn't really getting any-where in football, and I reached the point where I asked the manager either to sign me on as a full-time professional or let me go. I was ready to give up my ambitions of football fame, if I couldn't devote all my time to the job of making a success of kicking a ball around. Blackpool did sign me full-time, and that's how I started on the road to the First Division and England recognition.

Ian played for Barrow, and when they failed to gain re-election to the Fourth Division, two or three years back, it looked curtains for his hopes of a rise up the ladder. Barrow went into the Northern Premier League, and Ian was told that if he could find another club, they would let him move on. He wrote to half a dozen or so League clubs, but got nowhere – until Workington came along, and Barrow decided that he was worth a fee. Well, Workington paid up, and Ian was back in League football.

And so he arrived at Liverpool . . . five years after he had been down for a few days for a trial at Anfield. Now he's determined to make the break-through to first-team football as soon as possible and as a fellow-townsman, I hope he succeeds. But he knows he'll have to do it the hard way, because there's so much competition from so many talented players.

I started off by telling you how I love to go forward and have a pop at scoring goals. I've played midfield and I've played in the back four for Liverpool, dependent upon injuries and team requirements, and this is another thing about the club. You have to be versatile, and be prepared to cover for other players, whether they're out of action or whether it's during a game when our opponents are going on the attack. But not only that – the Liverpool lads are encouraged to do their own share of attacking, and while we have three front runners, it isn't a case of putting all the responsibility on their shoulders for getting the goals. Just because you're a midfield man, or even a full-back, it doesn't mean to say you haven't to have a go at scoring. And the proof is there for all to see, when you go through the players in the side who have tucked away scoring chances in matches.

Last season, Chris Lawler had a lengthy spell out of action, because of a cartilage operation – the first time he had been out of the side through injury since way back in 1965! How's that for consistency? And what about this for a scoring record, too? – Up to his injury, Chris had played 528 games for his one and only club, and had scored no fewer than sixty-one goals! The amazing thing, too, is that not one of those goals had come from the penalty spot . . . for Chris doesn't fancy taking spot-kicks!

Like myself, Tommy Smith, whose job has been in the back-four line, has scored close on half a century of goals, and Ian Callaghan, who seems likely to go on for ever, has scored around sixty goals for the club. Ian was a recognised winger, at one time – he was in England's 1966 World Cup squad – but he dropped back to midfield and really made his presence felt there, too. He has played well over 600 games for Liverpool, and 'Smithy' is coming up to the 500-match appearance mark.

Kevin Keegan finished last season with around fifty goals as a Liverpool player, and John Toshack has scored more than 130 goals in his career, including something like half a century since he joined Liverpool. Steve Heighway has scored more than thirty goals, Peter Cormack more than twenty, and Alec Lindsay, with more than a dozen, and Larry Lloyd, with about half a dozen, have got into the scoring act as well.

The season before last, when Liverpool won the League championship and the U.E.F.A. Cup, we played sixty-six competitive matches, and Larry Lloyd, Ian Callaghan and Chris Lawler played in them all. People such as Ray Clemence, Kevin Keegan, Steve Heighway and myself played in more than sixty of those games, and most of the other lads made close on sixty appearances. In fact, during that season, we used only sixteen

players – and one of those, goalkeeper Frank Lane, played only twice.

This is the sort of consistency, and scoring form spread around the side, which has made Liverpool such a formidable force in the First Division and in Europe – this is our 11th consecutive season in Europe – and the young players who have joined us in the last twelve months or so know that they have got to be right up to the mark, to stake their claim for promotion.

Of course, the fact that there are more and more young hopefuls waiting in the wings makes the regular first-teamers all the more determined that they won't surrender their places without a real battle, and the all-round competition can do nothing but good for the club.

And if there ever were a moment when you became tempted to take things easy, there's one man who simply wouldn't let that happen – manager Bill Shankly. You should see this fellow at our training sessions at Melwood . . . he joins in, and you'd think he was still playing for Scotland, or for his old club, Preston. I've got to know a lot of people inside football, managers and coaches, as well as players; but I'm convinced that there isn't another character in the game like the Liverpool manager.

I've seen him in all sorts of situations, and wondered how he manages to keep on going. Usually, he's geeing us up . . . and, now and again, when a match is over, you can tell he's really been out there on the park with us. When we survived a battering by Borussia Moenchengladbach in the U.E.F.A. Cup final two seasons ago, all the Liverpool lads were whacked, as they reached the dressing-room and went in to get bathed. We were literally drained of energy, for we had fought our hearts out to preserve a slender lead for more than half that game.

We had gone to Germany three goals ahead – and found ourselves two goals down, before half-time. The second half was a real backs-to-the-wall fight, and we finally achieved a 3–2 aggregate victory. As I say, when we got to the dressing-rooms, we were absolutely whacked . . . and 'the boss' looked just as drained as we were. He'd had to sit and suffer – and I'm sure he'd rather have been out on the park, playing for us instead of watching us trying to save the game. But within twenty minutes of the end, he was holding a Press conference and causing roars of laughter, as he cracked some of those famous jokes of his. Yes, Bill Shankly is the living proof of Liverpool's will to succeed. And you don't even mention the possibility of defeat, when he's around!

# My Route to the Top

## by TONY CURRIE

Not so many months ago, I read with interest what one of the most famous players in the game had to say about me. He's Mike Summerbee, the Manchester City and England winger, and I will say straight away that the professionals in the game know what a consistently good player Mike himself has been, throughout his career with Manchester City. He's skilled, fast, can take on and beat a man and he's brave. He's also played in the centre of the front line, as well as on the wing . . . and he was talking about me making a successful switch from midfield to the wing.

Now I've come to be regarded as a midfield player, although I know that Sheffield United manager Ken Furphy had me playing further upfield last season, for a spell, because he believes I can get a few goals. Mike Summerbee believes that I could make a name for myself as a winger . . . 'he's got the skill and the speed, and he's adaptable

enough to make a tremendous success of playing on the flank. He could become a great winger,' said Mike. All I can say is that when two of the top names in football have sufficient faith in you to talk about the job you can do, whether it's in midfield, up front or on the wing, then it's a real compliment, and I take it as such. The fact that I am rated an England international also helps me to believe in myself . . . and yet there was a time, believe me, when I thought that I was cut out to have a future in anything but professional football.

At one stage, when I was a few years younger, I went along to both Chelsea and Queen's Park Rangers for trials, hoping that as I was a London lad – I was born in Edgware – I would be taken on by one of these London clubs. But I obviously didn't make sufficient impression in the trials to warrant being offered terms, and I returned home

*Tony Currie ... a graduate to England international honours.*

disappointed. Six months later, I had all but given up the idea of playing football for a living.

I was working as a builder's labourer during the day – in fact, I was working from eight o'clock in the morning until six o'clock in the evening, and taking home less than a fiver in wages – and playing football on a Sunday, for relaxation. It was while I was playing in Sunday soccer that a Watford scout happened to spot me – and he felt that I had something which was worth keeping tabs on. I spent six weeks at Watford, and once again I was wondering if my career was going to come to a full stop before it had got going . . . then Watford decided to sign me on professional terms. I heaved a sigh of relief, because my Dad had been talking about

taking me away from Watford, since it seemed that things weren't going to pan out there, either.

Watford and I, as it turned out, did each other a favour, for I was in the first team by the time I had reached the age of eighteen, and I began to read that bigger clubs were keeping an eye on my progress. It's happened before – and when you read about yourself, you start to hope, yet you daren't let your hopes become too high, in case they are demolished. Not every player tipped to reach the top has made it, by a long way.

But Sheffield United, who have recruited more than their share of unknowns for modest sums – and signed quite a few players from Watford in the process – decided that I was a good enough investment to be worth a £26,000 transfer fee. I didn't know much about The Blades, at that time, although I did realise they were a First Division club, and I hadn't a moment's hesitation about signing on the dotted line. So far as I was concerned, it was my big chance – maybe the only one I'd get. So I didn't take much persuading to move from Watford to the city of steel.

I've got to admit now that if I'd known which way things were going to go for United that season, I might just have hesitated a little. Because that was the year they were celebrating fifty seasons of First Division football . . . and that was the season in which they were relegated to the Second Division. My First Division career hadn't lasted long.

However, when I look back, I cannot say that a spell in Second Division football appears to have done me any harm at all – indeed I was young enough to be learning something from every game that I played, and Watford was still a world removed from Bramall Lane. I'd played only two reserve matches for Sheffield United when they pitched me into the first team, and I made my debut against a London club, Tottenham Hotspur.

Suddenly, I was coming up against big-name players whom I'd only read about, or seen from a distance. Dave Mackay was still one of the strong men in the Spurs side, and Jimmy Greaves was still tucking away the scoring chances, even if he were approaching the end of his career. Martin Chivers, whom Spurs had signed for £125,000 from Southampton, was leading their front line, and he scored a very fine goal that day. But we managed to beat Tottenham, all the same, by the odd goal in five – and when I get talking to Sheffield United fans and my debut crops up in the conversation, some of them still reckon that I haven't played a better game for The Blades yet.

A couple of years ago, there was a chance that I might have been moving on from 'The Lane' . . . back to London . . . and that the clubs most likely to be bidding for me were Tottenham and Arsenal. There were also stories that Manchester United and Everton were in the hunt for my signature, and I have to confess that I began to feel a bit restive. I was still ambitious, and although I was grateful for the fact that Sheffield United had given me my chance to hit the big-time, I felt that perhaps I might win

honours more quickly with another, more fashionable club. It took a bit of talking to sort things out, but eventually I decided that all was not gold that glittered, and I agreed to sign a new contract for The Blades. It was clear that they had ambitious plans for the future themselves, and they convinced me that I was one of the key men in those plans.

By then, United had climbed out of the Second Division, and I had made my mark at representative level, for I was an England Under-23 player, and hopeful of breaking through to the full international team. I managed it, too, on a close-season tour, and I played in matches against Austria, Poland and Italy last year. That game against Poland, of course, was one which ended in heartbreak for all the England lads, and I can still see the dressing-room scene now, when we knew we had failed to qualify for the 1974 World Cup, because we had only managed to draw against the Poles. Some of the lads were in tears, and Sir Alf had a difficult time consoling them.

My first game had been against Russia, and I was pretty satisfied with my performance. I don't think I did too badly in my other outings, either. But I know that you have to keep on turning in top-class displays to nail down a place as an England regular. And certainly our manager at Bramall Lane, Ken Furphy, has been giving me some pep-talks about my future at club and international level. In fact, he's gone on record as saying that he believes I can finish up by skippering England, and being an international for years to come. I just hope I can live up to his great expectations!

Our paths crossed again, of course, when Ken Furphy left Blackburn Rovers to take over at 'The Lane'. He had been the manager at Watford when I signed for Sheffield United, and now he's my boss again. He has made it quite plain to all of us, as well, that he is as ambitious for The Blades to go places as anyone else at the club, and that's a heartening thing. I've had five years and more at Bramall Lane now, and I would love us to win one of the major prizes in the game.

I'd just like to add a few words here about another player at United – winger Alan Woodward. He's been one of the most consistent players not just in the club, but in the country, since he made his first-team debut at eighteen against Liverpool. He's still only twenty-seven now, and he's still scoring goals regularly – in fact, he's been one of our leading marksmen at the club for the past few seasons, and his play always seems to reach the same high standard.

I began this article by telling you what Mike Summerbee had said about my chances of becoming a top-class winger, and, as I said, I appreciate the compliment, which I know was sincere. I can tell you this much – if I ever do set out with the fixed idea of becoming a wing man, I won't need to look any further for lessons in the art than Mike Summerbee and Alan Woodward. In so many respects, these two fellows are the same, and they have both given years of loyal service to their respective clubs.

Alan is a Yorkshire lad, while Mike was signed by Manchester City from Swindon. Alan cost nowt, as they say in Yorkshire, Mike cost £35,000. But even that fee has been chicken-feed, considering the service Mike has given City. Both these players have been regular first-teamers virtually since the day they made their debuts, and I am sure that it's going to take somebody rather special to oust either of them.

Many people have admitted that they have been puzzled as to why Mike Summerbee hasn't won more international caps, and certainly the lads at 'The Lane' would give a vote of confidence to Alan Woodward, who hasn't been capped even at Under-23 level – although there's still time for him to make the jump straight into the full international squad. Like Mike Summerbee, Alan Woodward rarely goes missing from the team through injury; but I know Mike won't argue too much if I say that Alan probably has a better scoring record, for he almost always comes up with anything from a dozen to fifteen goals in a season, and that's a good record for a winger.

But if Alan Woodward has made a habit of scoring goals, over the years, I'll tell you something else – there has been the odd occasion when he's been given the job of stopping 'em, too. One time was in a game against Leeds United, when our 'keeper, Alan Hodgkinson, went off injured, and Alan Woodward was handed the goalkeeper's jersey. He spent eighty minutes of that game between the posts, and he defied everything that Leeds could throw at him. And as United scored a goal, that meant The Blades finished up as the winners.

I know Alan still nurses the ambition to make the England team, and nothing would please me more than to be there with him. He's been a great team-mate at Sheffield United, and I know he would do a good job in the white jersey, too. As for me, I'm keeping my fingers crossed that there are plenty more caps to come from where the last few have been awarded. And I'll be trying my hardest to claim an England spot. After all, there is another World Cup in 1978!

*It must have been easier playing the game than watching it, especially as a manager – that seems to be Jackie Charlton's mood, judging from his expression as he scans the action from the bench at Middlesbrough.*

# BIG JACK AND BROTHER BOB

The Compton brothers, Leslie and Denis; the Robledo brothers, George and Ted; the Charlton brothers, Jack and Bobby. These men made their names in big-time football as players. Between them, they won international honours and played in Cup finals. But probably no one will ever outstrip the two Charltons for fame in the game. Big Jack played for Leeds United and England, 'wor Bobby' played for Manchester United and England . . . and they were together in the same team which won the World Cup for England, in 1966. Each man played hundreds of games for his respective club – between them, they clocked up around 1,300 – and each man decided to hang up his boots at the end of the season of 1972–73.

Bobby Charlton, who had won a European Cup medal, F.A. Cup and League-championship medals with Manchester United, helped them stave off relegation that season. When he hung up his boots as a player, he had scored 199 League goals for United, and become the idol of youngsters all over the country. His sportsmanship, his modesty, his sharp-shooting . . . all these qualities had brought him fame, admiration, deep respect. Like his brother, he had also been named Footballer of the Year – and he had won the coveted European Footballer of the Year award as well.

Big Jack was the fellow who stopped 'em. He didn't score goals, for his job was to block the route to Leeds United's goal. And he did this with tremendous effect, in a career spanning twenty years at Elland Road. In his last season, he had a testimonial match – as did brother Bobby – and he helped to bring on his successor, Gordon McQueen.

For many weeks, there had been speculation that Jack Charlton was destined for the world of soccer management, and finally it was announced that he would be taking charge of Second Division Middlesbrough. Brother Bobby was an obvious target for a club seeking a manager, and his name was linked with Preston, also in the Second Division. Preston got their man, as did Boro' . . . and everyone speculated on what would happen, now that they were in opposition once more, this time as managers.

Oddly enough, one man who played alongside them with England, and as a Manchester United club-mate with Bobby, got to know at first-hand what both men were like as managers. For, in turn, he played for Middlesbrough under Jack Charlton, and for Preston under Bobby. His name: Nobby Stiles, one never to be forgotten when thinking of England and that 1966 World Cup triumph.

Nobby had shared in Manchester United's glories, and this Collyhurst-born player finally left Old Trafford to join Middlesbrough. He was there when big Jack arrived at Ayresome, to take

*Smiles all round, as Bobby Charlton embarks on his first managerial job, with Preston North End.*

82

over the managerial reins . . . and a few months later, he returned to his beloved Manchester, signed for Preston, and went to work for Bobby. Nobby had never really settled since he moved from Manchester, but big Jack was reluctant to let him go. However, the day came when he accepted the inevitable, and Nobby became a Preston player.

By then, Boro' were clearly showing that they were going to be in the fore-front of the promotion race. Preston were some way behind. Jack Charlton, who couldn't have learned more than he did from Don Revie about the art of management, also had his own ideas, and he put them into practice. Nobby Stiles was convinced before he left Ayresome Park that Jack would steer Boro' to promotion. His verdict: 'Boro' were a sound Second Division side, before Jack went there; but he gave them something they hadn't got before . . . patience.' Boro' had been able to score a few goals, but they had also conceded some. Nobby said: 'Under Jack, they learned how to bide their time. How to play the waiting game, snatch a goal – and make sure the opposition didn't catch them on the rebound.' Nobby rated Alan Foggon, a £10,000 signing, as one of the bargain buys, and Middlesbrough snapped up Bobby Murdoch, a tremendously experienced player, when he was freed by Glasgow Celtic. And Boro' pushed their way to the top of the Second Division table, and defied their rivals to dislodge them. By the start of 1974, Boro' were five points clear, and they strolled into the First Division.

Preston, on the other hand, went down to Division 3, after a brief spell when they had threatened to make a bold showing in the promotion fight. They had signed David Sadler from Manchester United, too, and Ray Treacy from Swindon, and Francis Burns – another one-time Old Trafford player – from Southampton. But it was clear that Bobby was going to have a bit of a battle on his hands. Some people said that Bobby was finding out, for the first time, the rough edge of soccer. There were those, too, who believed that Bobby's life at the top with United, and his own, quiet personality, might find him not too well fitted for the business of being not only the boss, but a hard task-master into the bargain, when necessary.

Nobby Stiles didn't agree. 'Bobby knows what he wants from his players, and he knows how to do his job. He's been learning, to some extent, but you can take it from me that he's got more determination and can handle matters much better than some folk gave him credit for. He's not soft.' That was the verdict of Manchester City chairman Peter Swales, too, who was on Bobby Charlton's testimonial committee, and who had got to know him well at first hand. 'Somewhere, deep down, there's a streak of steel in Bobby Charlton,' said Peter Swales. 'It didn't seem to be apparent when he was a player, but I have been a little bit surprised by the way he has coped with the responsibilities of management. That streak of steel will stand him in good stead, all right.'

Big Jack and brother Bobby are different physically, and different in some ways temperamentally. Big Jack often says what he thinks – and even if you don't agree with him, he generally makes sense. He doesn't flatter people, speaks his mind . . . and that doesn't go down well with everyone. But there's no malice behind the words, and the sting is often taken out of them by a friendly grin. Jack can be hard, and he certainly gives the impression of being positive, both in his opinions and in his actions.

Bobby is the quieter of the two, by far. He thinks a lot, but doesn't always say what he's thinking. One player who had been a team-mate of Bobby's at Old Trafford once said that he was never quite sure that he knew him, really. When Jack and Bobby were players, they often came up in opposition – and big Jack didn't stand on ceremony when they clashed. But between the two, there has always existed a mutual respect, and this has grown with the years. Typically, though, neither man expects favours from the other, as rival managers.

One man who came to know Jack Charlton very well is Bobby Collins, formerly a star with Everton and Leeds, and now on the coaching side of the game. Bobby says: 'Big Jack's attitude has changed over the years – and I know he won't mind me saying that, for he speaks his mind himself. At one time, when he was a player, he went his own way. But he was shrewd enough to realise that good advice can be beneficial, if you're prepared to listen. And he decided that he would listen. In that respect, I'm sure Don Revie must have had more influence with him than anyone else.

'Jack achieved a great deal of fame, as a player, and when he and Leeds started going places, it was success all the way. When he was appointed the manager of Middlesbrough, I felt that here was another kind of challenge to him . . . and it can happen with anyone: you can be a terrific success in a new kind of job, or you can be a flop. I thought he would be a success, because he'd learned to listen, although he was still prepared to back his own judgment. Jack will talk to anyone – he's got that something about him called personality. He believes in what he thinks, and he can put it across to others.

'In fact, I don't think he has had the publicity he deserves, since he went to Middlesbrough. The results he achieved spoke for themselves, but it WAS his first job in football management. And it's only when you get talking to people in the game that you discover people have a high opinion of his coaching abilities, for instance – that's an activity the fans never see, of course. He had had no experience as a manager, but he wakened things up at Boro' – and I think he's been a marvellous advert, not just for himself, but in proving that new-comers can make their way in football management.'

Bobby Collins, a one-time Scotland international, is cast in the same mould as Jack Charlton, so maybe he's got a closer insight into what makes the big fellow tick than most, especially as they were team-mates at Elland Road for so long. Bobby didn't get to know Bobby Charlton well, other than as an opponent. 'I got the impression that Bobby was much more reserved than Jack, although he had had just as much success as a player. But I think Bobby's character has shown through, too, in the face of a few setbacks since he went into management, and the experience of his first season as a team boss should stand him in good stead.'

There's a long way to go before the Charlton brothers, Jack and Bobby, get to the very top of the tree in their new roles, of course. But though they may differ in their approach to their respective jobs, it seems that, given time, they can become just as big names in management as they were on the playing side. Certainly, they have both been serving the right sort of apprenticeship . . . and in men like Don Revie and Sir Matt Busby, they couldn't have had better tutors, or examples to follow.

85

# Well, what DO you know?

*Answers are on page 117.*

You think you know your football? Then test yourself with this Soccer quiz... 96 questions about the players, the clubs, the countries, the competitions – everything, in fact, concerning the game which, as Billy Bremner says, still remains the greatest in the world. Are you ready? Then get set, GO...

**1.** Name the last two brothers to play in the same F.A. Cup final.

**2.** Name the last player to score a hat-trick in an F.A. Cup semi-final.

**3.** Name a First Division player who has played in the same forward line as his present manager. Here's a clue... the player is now an international, and a midfield man.

**4.** Name the goalkeeper who was on the losing side in an F.A. Cup final at Wembley – but didn't concede a goal.

**5.** Name the team that played in the F.A. Cup, never lost a game – but never won the Cup.

**6.** What was so unusual about the referee in the 1956 F.A. Cup final, and what was his name?

**7.** Name a former Liverpool player who holds an F.A. Cup scoring record with another club. A clue... he's cost £200,000 in a transfer deal, and has played for five clubs – and had three quick-fire transfers, none of them of his own seeking.

**8.** Got the name? Well, what was the record he set?

**9.** How many caps did Gordon Banks win, when playing for England?

**10.** Name the footballer who played in no fewer than five different World Cup competitions.

**11.** Name five teams outside Britain who have beaten England at Wembley.

**12.** Name the four clubs who have completed the double of winning the League championship and the F.A. Cup in one season.

**13.** What is England's record defeat, in an international match?

86

**14.** Name a player, capped for England since the war, but born in South Africa.

**15.** Name a player, born in South Africa, who is now a British subject and playing for a First Division club.

**16.** Which club has appeared in most F.A. Cup finals?

**17.** Which Third Division ground was used in the 1966 World Cup?

**18.** Name the last non-League team to win the F.A. Cup.

**19.** Name the last Fourth Division club to play at Anfield against Liverpool. A clue . . . it was in the F.A. Cup last season.

**20.** Name the player who made his debut for his club in an F.A. Cup final at Wembley.

**21.** Which famous football club lost many of its players in an air crash in 1958?

**22.** Which famous club lost many of its players in an air crash in 1949?

**23.** Name two clubs which have each scored six goals in F.A. Cup finals.

**24.** Name a player who scored six goals himself in an F.A. Cup-tie . . . and still didn't finish on the winning side, that day.

**25.** When was the last time a team won the First Division championship on goal average?

**26.** Which team won the F.A. Cup and promotion in the same season?

**27.** Which team won the League championship and a European trophy in the same season?

**28.** Which team has played most European Cup finals at Wembley?

**29.** Name the last German-born player to play in an F.A. Cup final at Wembley.

**30.** Which club holds the record for the most consecutive F.A. Cup defeats?

**31.** Who scored Glasgow Celtic's goals, in their European Cup-final victory over Inter-Milan in 1967?

**32.** What was the score when Manchester United beat Benfica in the 1968 European Cup final?

**33.** Name the manager who managed two different League Cup-winning sides.

**34.** Name the manager who took two different teams to Wembley, in the League Cup final, in successive seasons.

**35.** Name the manager who steered his team to the championship of the First, Second and Third divisions.

**36.** Which South African player scored the winning goal in an F.A. Cup final at Wembley, since the war?

**37.** Which player scored his club's 6,000th League goal? – A clue, he's a Scot . . . and the club is one of the crack Scottish clubs.

**38.** Four Second Division clubs have reached the F.A. Cup final since the war. Can you name them?

**39.** Four clubs reached the semi-finals of the F.A. Cup, as Third Division clubs. Can you name them?

**40.** Which player has played in the most F.A. Cup finals?

**41.** Which was the first Russian club to tour Britain, after the war?

**42.** Which team were the first winners of the European Cup?

**43.** Can you name two clubs whose grounds are known as St. James's Park?

**44.** Can you name four clubs who are known by the nickname of The Robins?

**45.** Which two clubs are known as The Valiants?

**46.** Where would you find the Nep-stadion, the Wiener stadium, and the Bernabeau stadium?

**47.** Sunderland won the F.A. Cup two seasons ago – but have they ever won the League championship?

**48.** Which was the first major trophy won by Stoke City?

**49.** Who was the first teenager to cost £100,000 in a transfer deal between English clubs?

**50.** Which clubs have reached the final of the League Cup most times?

**51.** Who were the first winners of the Football League Cup?

**52.** Which League Cup final drew its first 100,000 crowd?

**53.** Which player came on as substitute in a League Cup final at Wembley – and scored the winning goal?

**54.** Can you name a club which appeared in successive League Cup finals – and lost, on each occasion?

**55.** Which was the first English club to compete in the European Cup?

**55.** Name a player who signed for Cardiff City last season, to bring the total of League clubs for whom he had played to eight.

**57.** Which club did Alan Ashman manage, in between leaving West Brom and returning as team boss at Carlisle?

**58.** Alan Ashman took West Brom to the F.A. Cup final in 1968 – whom did they beat?

**59.** When West Brom went to the final of the Football League Cup, in 1970, they lost – against whom?

**60.** Who was the first player to have been involved in three separate, £100,000 transfer deals?

**61.** How many League goals did Bobby Charlton score – 109, 159 or 199?

**62.** Which player has cost the record fee between British clubs?

**63.** Which player became the first £100,000 goalkeeper to join an English First Division club?

**64.** Can you name five players who went from English soccer to Italian football?

**65.** Can you name two international goalkeepers who are now managers in the English League?

**66.** Two brothers who play for the same First Division club ... names, please.

**67.** Who became the youngest player to score 100 League goals?

**68.** Can you name the youngest player to appear in an F.A. Cup final?

**69.** Malcolm Macdonald is a feared marksman with Newcastle today ... but which player scored six goals on his debut for Newcastle, back in 1946? A clue ... he was known as 'The Clown Prince of Football'.

**70.** Who was the first Footballer of the Year?

**71.** Which players have won the Footballer of the Year award twice?

**72.** Denis Law and Joe Baker both played for the same Italian club, at one stage in their careers. Which club was it?

**73.** With which League club did Rodney Marsh kick off his career?

**74.** Can you name an international

centre-forward, still playing, who has been with four Lancashire clubs?

**75.** Norwich City's longest-serving player, who made 622 appearances for the club between 1947 and 1964, later managed the Canaries for a spell. Who is he?

**76.** Norwich were beaten finalists in the Football League Cup two seasons ago, and semi-finalists last season, when they lost to Wolves. But have they ever won the League Cup?

**77.** For which club did Norwich City's present manager, John Bond, play?

**78.** The World Cup has been and gone. Can you say how old Pele was, when he played in the 1958 tournament, in Sweden?

**79.** Brazil's Jairzinho scored the goal that beat England in Mexico, in 1970. How many goals did he score altogether in that tournament – five, six or seven?

**80.** Which was the first £100,000 transfer deal between Scottish clubs?

**81.** What was the name of the player involved in the first £1,000 transfer?

**82.** Denis Law joined Manchester City on a free transfer last season. It was his second spell with the Maine Road club. How much did he cost when they signed him the first time?

**83.** Which club did they sign him from then?

**84.** Up to the 1974 World Cup, Brazil had won the tournament three times, and two other countries had each won the competition twice. Can you name those countries?

**85.** Had West Germany ever won the World Cup, before they became host nation in the last tournament?

**86.** In which countries has the World Cup competition been held, since its inception in 1930? Remember, it comes round every four years . . .

**87.** Gunter Netzer joined Real Madrid last season, for a reputed fee of around £300,000. Which was his previous club?

**88.** Which club did Johann Cruyff, the famous scoring ace with Dutch champions and European Cup-holders Ajax, join last season?

**89.** Which club has set a record for the number of players who have won the European Footballer of the Year award? A clue . . . it's a famous English club.

**90.** Which of its players won the coveted award?

**91.** Can you name a First Division manager who has won the Manager of the Year award, and who also won the Footballer of the Year award, when he was a player?

**92.** Can you name three pairs of brothers who went into football management?

**93.** England have never yet won the European Nations Cup. What has been their best placing, to date?

**94.** Has any country won the European Nations Cup more than once, so far?

**95.** The first game England played under the managership of Sir Alf Ramsey was in the Nations Cup, in 1963. Whom did England play?

**96.** Can you remember the result?

# MAN in the MIDDLE

## by GORDON HILL

*He's the man they call the 'players' referee' – Gordon Hill, Lancashire-born and now a headmaster at a high school in Leicester. On the field of action, he doesn't come the heavy-handed school-master with players . . . he chats them up, and maintains discipline with the aid of repartee. Once, he was a footballer him-self – a centre-half in amateur soccer. But injury cut short his playing days, and he became a referee. He's handled some of the biggest games, at home and abroad, and here he talks about games . . . and about the star players of soccer. They all know him – and he knows them all.*

I'd like to make one thing clear, at the start: only the best referees reach the Football League list; there are NO bad referees at this level, even if their per-formances sometimes vary. I'm con-vinced that British referees are still the best in the world . . . and I'm absolutely certain that you would find the players in this country agreeing with this view.

The first time I refereed a First Division game, my knees were knocking – and no wonder, for the match was at Anfield. They say that until you've refereed a game at Anfield, you haven't really refereed. Well, I can tell you that the atmosphere there is always tremen-dous, and often electric. I was keyed up, as I prepared to toss the coin. Ron Yeats, the centre-half that Liverpool manager Bill Shankly called 'The Colos-sus', was skippering the home side, and he towered over even my lean, six-foot frame. He was able to look down on me, as he ruffled my hair and said, smilingly: 'Best of luck in your first big game, ref.' It was a nice gesture which I appreciated at the time, and I have never forgotten since. Players can be good guys, even if sometimes they lose their way in the heat of the action.

The game hadn't been going long before a small dog raced on the field. I

90

managed to catch it, and as I carried it off, the Kop chorus roared: 'Ee-aye-addio . . . the ref.'s got a dog!'

Suddenly, I got the feeling that the fans were in sympathy with me, and I began to enjoy the game. I've enjoyed many more games since that day, and I've got to know a lot of the players very well, as skilled footballers and as persons. I think that over the years, we've worked out an understanding of each other, and of each other's problems.

I remember an Anglo-Italian tournament game between Lazio and Manchester United, and things got a bit rough, to say the least. There were 50,000 fanatical Italian fans baying for blood, and I'll admit it – at the end of the game, I felt that perhaps I hadn't been as firm as I might have been. But I'll never forget the wonderful self-control of the Manchester United players, especially Bobby Charlton, George Graham and Willie Morgan. They were magnificent, and set a real example to their team-mates.

A few months later, when I had got my nerve back, I was in charge of another match which was full of tension. Liverpool were playing Leeds at Anfield on the Easter Monday, and the result of that game could virtually settle the championship of the First Division. It just about did, too, for Liverpool won, 2–0, and that dashed Leeds' hopes of making a late breakthrough for the title. Liverpool won the championship – and, for good measure, the U.E.F.A. Cup.

As I drove down the East Lancashire Road towards Anfield, I got caught up in the procession of traffic coming off the motorway from Leeds. Three hours before the game began, the fans were queuing up to get inside the ground. Two hours before kick-off time, the gates were closed, with more than 55,000 people inside. And when I saw the players, most of them looked a bit gaunt, for they knew only too well what this match meant to them.

It turned out to be a tremendous performance, all the way round. Once, when things looked like getting a bit heated between two players, I nipped in, putting an arm around each of them, and walking them away from trouble. I reminded them that it would be better for everyone if they cooled it – and they did. Tommy Smith wasn't too happy on one occasion, when he reckoned he'd been fouled, but I ran past him and told him to get off his backside and get on with the game. Smithy, like the good professional he is, didn't argue the toss. He grinned, and did as he was told. He's my kind of player.

When Liverpool tucked away their second goal, a couple of their players raced to face the Kop, to salute the fans and be saluted. I couldn't help sharing their moment of joy . . . I just went back to the centre of the field and sat on the ball until play could start again. I believe a referee has to give players a bit of rope, at times, and – if necessary – indulge in a bit of quick repartee. When a player starts 'rabbiting' at the ref., a sharp, snappy retort can often take the string out of things. Tommy Smith once paid me the compliment of saying I talk like a professional and operate like one.

*Keeping a watchful eye on the auld enemy . . . that's Scotland skipper Billy Bremner. And Martin Chivers, playing this for England, not Spurs, knows that it won't be easy to make a scoring chance out of this situation.*

I'll return the compliment, for in my book, Smithy is one of the most professional footballers in the game.

So is Billy Bremner. He's had a bit of a reputation for talking back, in the past, but I've always got on well with him, by and large. And I've talked back to him, sometimes. I've seen Billy almost gritting his teeth, at times, in his determination not to be provoked into retaliation. I remember one occasion when he was fouled, and it could have been a nasty injury, but fortunately the little Scot was soon on his feet again – although he was hopping mad. But I kept the trainer on the field a bit longer than necessary, to continue the treatment . . . and to give Billy the chance to cool down. It worked, too.

And when Leeds had been beaten by Liverpool in that Easter Monday match, I had to admire United's skipper, for he called to his own men to form a guard of honour for the Liverpool lads as they left the field.

Sometimes, I make a point of thanking players for not getting stuck into each other. There was one game where two of them were getting ready to square up, then each of them thought better of it, and began to grin. The game carried on, and as I ran past them, I grinned, too, and said: 'Thanks, lads.'

Manchester City's Mike Summerbee doesn't talk too much – except when he thinks he's being given too much stick from an opponent. But Franny Lee . . . now, you get a constant stream of conversation from him. I remember a Spurs–Manchester City game, when Franny broke through into the penalty area, then shot wide. I had a sly dig, as I walked past him: 'Franny lad, in your pomp you'd have eaten that!' I said. He answered with a few choice words, we grinned at each other – and got cracking on the game again.

Rodney Marsh once took a waist-high pass, but couldn't control it with his foot . . . so, he caught the ball, rugby style, raced 20 yards and touched down. The crowd roared, and I chuckled as I said: 'Aye, it's just about your game, too!' Rod didn't take the huff, though – he can take a joke.

Sometimes a bit of the showbiz style pays off in soccer, and I don't think it ever does any harm to show that you're ready to share a bit of backchat with the players. It helps to get rid of the tension for everyone. And referees suffer from tension, just as much as professional footballers.

In my first season on the list, I refereed a game between Halifax and Southport. And I had what is known as a stinker. In fact, by the end of the game, I was coming to the conclusion that refereeing wasn't my cup of tea after all, and wondering if I should write a letter of resignation to League headquarters. I was so bad in that game that I'm sure I didn't receive any marks from either club. But I got over it, and I wasn't fired – and before the end of that season, I'd refereed Southport and been back to Halifax again. Since then, I've refereed many big games – in Berlin, in Rome, in the F.A. Cup, League Cup, and top First Division matches. And while I've often been self-critical, because I know I *have* made mistakes during matches,

I've felt it an honour to be chosen week after week to handle matches in English League football.

Liverpool manager Bill Shankly is one of *the* characters in football, take it from me. They tell dozens of stories about him. He preaches physical fitness, he preaches fair play, he preaches the will to win. When things have gone well for you, as a referee, he's the first to congratulate you; when you've dropped a clanger, he doesn't say a word to you . . . but, as he walks past you, his eyes show what he's feeling. And you get the message. He knows you've boobed – and you know that he knows.

Once, Bill Shankly invited myself and a pal to lunch with him in his den under the stand at Anfield. For an hour and a half, all we heard was the story of his great team . . . and there was not the slightest doubt about his sincerity, or of his dedication to football. Those were ninety of the greatest minutes of my life, and they didn't happen on the field of play.

Arsenal's Alan Ball doesn't know what it is to think about losing, or to be frightened during a game. But in one match I refereed, he was laid out cold for fully a minute by a really tough tackle. When he began to come to, his first words were: 'Who hit me?'

I took the heat out of that situation with a snappy remark. 'Didn't you see that No. 11 bus going down the Kings Road?' Slowly, Bally began to grin . . .

and then he started laughing outright.

A couple of seasons ago, I refereed the Norwich City–Chelsea League Cup semi-final. Norwich, who had won at Stamford Bridge in the first leg, were looking outright winners with four minutes to go in the return game at Carrow Road. But the fog really began to blot out play, and I felt I had no alternative but to abandon the game.

I had to go back to Norwich for the second attempt, and the atmosphere was tense, for Chelsea clearly had been given a reprieve. However, Norwich came good again, and they duly marched on to Wembley. But two weeks after that second game, I was back at Carrow Road, for an F.A. Cup-tie against Leeds. There were queues of fans, of course, and as I walked into the ground, I heard one of the wisecracks from someone who had obviously recognised me: 'Oh, it's Hill again . . . is it true they're putting your name on the housing list here?'

Yes, you get cracks from the fans, as well as from the players, now and again. And I like to think that I can keep my cool and put a bit of laughter into the game at times, for I really do believe that this is the sort of thing which helps to make football a game, rather than a battle. And I believe, also, that football should always be striving to produce entertainment for the spectators who have paid good money to watch a match.

# Killing 'em to be kind

## by DEREK IBBOTSON

At the age of fifteen, I was convinced that I would eventually become a professional footballer, and play for Huddersfield Town. I suppose that schoolboys who feel they have talent always have dreams such as this; but my ambitions, I will confess, stemmed mainly from the fact, not that I possessed so much talent, but because I knew for certain that I had fantastic stamina . . . and determination.

My father went along to watch me in a school match, and from his after-match comment, it was pretty clear that he had decided my future lay elsewhere than in professional soccer. 'Son', he said, 'you have a fantastic amount of energy, and you cover more ground than two players. But you haven't got much idea.'

That was straight enough Yorkshire talk, and as it turned out, football's loss became athletics' gain. But little did my father or myself realise that it would take me to the age of thirty-four before I DID break into professional football . . . and not as a player, but as a fitness coach to Manchester City.

As football has developed through the years, so the roles of the players have become more marked, and the ideas about the way they should achieve and maintain fitness have become more advanced. For instance, take the midfield player: the tremendous determination and stamina required by players such as Billy Bremner and Colin Bell meant that footballers had to undertake the sort of training endured by Olympic athletes.

And that is probably why I first received the call from Manchester City, when Malcolm Allison was at Maine Road, in October, 1966. He was assistant manager in those days, and he and Joe Mercer formed a tremendously successful partnership, as Manchester City went on to win honours – promotion, the championship of the First Division, the F.A. Cup, the Football League Cup and the European Cup-winners Cup.

Joe Lancaster, the former long-distance runner and coach, was also at Maine-road, and so I found myself

95

alongside someone whose mind ran on similar lines to my own. At that time, City had just gained promotion from the Second Division, but they were struggling a bit in the lower reaches of the First Division table. Yet there was no doubt at all that they were ambitious to climb right to the top.

So we decided to launch the City players on a Monday-morning 'killer programme', to sort out the ones who were going to make it with the team in the days of ambition and achievement which Joe and Malcolm envisaged ahead.

The idea of choosing a Monday morning was to get the players back into working shape after their relaxing week-end. And when you've been enjoying yourself after the 90-minute match action of the previous Saturday, that Monday-morning feeling doesn't normally dispose you to jump to it and go in for a tough training session.

Any way, we met the players, and had a short discussion with them, telling them what was in our minds for their 'treatment' – and their ultimate benefit – and they seemed to take things in their stride. They appeared to be quite happy about our plans, and their comments were as normal as those of any athlete.

It was very handy having Malcolm Allison in charge of the training, because he was the type of man who made sure that the schedule was carried out to the letter. We worked on the theory that if a top athlete could get through a steady morning stint of between forty-five minutes and an hour, and a tough evening session of around ninety min-

utes – almost every day of the week, mind you – then professional footballers would be able to stand a very hard and gruelling 90-minute session on a Monday morning.

After the first few sessions, the players' greatest moan was that they could not really recover in time for the following Saturday's match! To quote comedian Eric Morecambe (who is also a director of Luton Town) . . . RUBBISH!

We began in a steady fashion, with a plan to work up slowly through the weeks until the players could accept a much bigger load. The aim for the first season was to improve the fitness level of the players, so that they could just manage to survive in the First Division – they did this, all right, because they finished in 15th place.

The idea for the pre-season training of 1967–68 was to try to improve the all-round stamina of the team without losing any speed – and, in fact, if possible, to increase a player's speed by extra fitness. This idea worked, too, in some instances.

It is certainly a fallacy that the only way to improve a footballer's stamina is by going on long, boring runs round the outside of the pitch. This method of stamina training used to blunt the players' enthusiasm and it could also harm their speed.

We were fortunate in having a very good training area to use at Wythenshawe Park, on the outskirts of Manchester. There were about four miles of good grassland running through the trees and small golf course, and we also had the use of a cinder track in the centre of the park.

I always insisted on a very good warm-up of around a mile and a half to two miles, followed by fifteen minutes of loosening up and of exercises to make the body supple. We would then start the training session with a mixture of slow and fast running, through the trees and across parkland, over varying distances, covering three or four miles. Then it was a case of back to the track to do some interval work and some very fast running on the track.

The main distance was a 220-yard stretch. We did a fast 220 yards in about thirty seconds, with a jog of 220 yards 'rest' taking a couple of minutes or so. We did about eight or ten of these sessions, then finished off with four or six flat-out sprints over 50 yards, starting on a word of command. And to round it all off, we did a steady jog for four or five minutes to ease out the lactic acid build-up in the muscle system.

The programme was varied almost every week, to build up the players gradually and to prevent them from becoming bored.

And over the next few years, Manchester City won the honours I mentioned earlier – League, F.A. Cup, League Cup and Cup-winners Cup – so the experiment dreamed up by Malcolm Allison had obviously turned out to be successful.

Another club wasn't slow to catch on to the idea that there might be something in the kind of 'treatment' I had been dishing out to footballers, and Stoke City became my next port of call. Here, we have been using the same principles, but instead of all the playing staff working together, coach Alan A'Court splits them into three groups. One group does the running with me, the second group does a weight-and-fitness circuit, and the third group concentrates on ball skills in the gymnasium or on the practice ground with Gordon Banks, Alan A'Court or George Eastham.

The groups switch around twice, and spend thirty to forty minutes on each section of this training, which is therefore spread over ninety minutes to a couple of hours, altogether. By using all the players, from ground staff lads to first-team men, everyone is brought through on the same system, and so moving up in the club becomes much easier and requires less adjustment, as the juniors make their progress towards the top.

We work out at various times at the ground, or at the Keele University sports complex – and we also use Trentham Gardens, which comprises a large, hilly forested area and a golf course. We do a lot of hill running at a fastish pace, and the really fast running comes on the golf course.

I have no doubts at all that doing really hard training in such beautiful surroundings makes it so much easier – even if the lads being put through their paces don't always agree with me! But then, as I often tell them, it's a case of killing them, to be kind . . .

# Sweet Sixteen!

## by Billy Bremner

Sixteen years is a long time, in the life of a professional footballer – but that's how long I've been at Leeds United. And I hope to be there for a few more years yet! A lot has happened in those sixteen years – in the early days, when Leeds were a struggling Second Division club, there were a couple of times when I wanted to return home across the Border, but thank goodness I was talked out of it...

When it comes to the partnership between manager Don Revie and myself, it may surprise you to learn that it began on the field of play, because when I made my first-team debut for Leeds, against Chelsea at Stamford Bridge, I was out on the right wing – and Don Revie was my inside-forward partner.

He and I roomed together the night before the game; he looked after me all the way, and talked football to me all the time. And I suppose it was as early as that that I came to realise just what a

deep thinker this fellow was, so far as the professional game was concerned. Later, he became the manager of Leeds – more than once, in those early days, I did some baby-sitting for the boss and his wife – and together, we've gone up in the world with Leeds United. Now Don Revie's children are grown up, and there's no need for baby-sitters... and Leeds United have grown up, too. More than that – at last, we have become recognised as a truly great club. But it has been hard graft, with many disappointments, as well as achievements, on the way.

Of course, I am delighted – for myself and my team-mates – that Leeds last season were hailed as a great side. But even more, I was delighted for all that it meant to Don Revie, the man who has guided us for so long.

When the boss started out in management, he was very much on trial, and he knew it. There were setbacks in those

98

early days, but HE knew what he wanted. For he confided that though Leeds were struggling, and short of a bit of brass, at that, his ambition was for them to become the NEW Manchester United of British football. United – the Manchester club, I mean – were at the pinnacle, and they were regarded as the glamour club (rightly so) of soccer. The players in their side were just about all internationals; their style of football was exciting, entertaining, sweet-flowing. Don Revie wasn't going to be satisfied until Leeds United could match, and even surpass, the standard set by the other United.

Well, I believe that we have now achieved our goal. We have had a team of internationals for quite a while, and although people may have labelled us as failures, at times, in the past, we have soldiered on. And now, we have not just been hailed as a great side which stands comparison with others that have gone before; we have won over the fans, both at Leeds and around the country. And this is perhaps the sweetest music of all, for us to hear.

When you get managers like Joe Harvey of Newcastle, Noel Cantwell of Peterborough, Bill McGarry of Wolves, and others singing your praises, and calling you a great team, then you know you've been handed the accolade by the men who are in business as your fiercest competitors. When you get the fans rolling up, at home and away, so that you can bank on gates of around 40,000 – and at a time when attendances are dwindling generally – then you know you've really cracked it.

And, as I say, most of all, I'm delighted for Don Revie. Because when things have gone awry for us in the past, when we've been tempted to hang our heads, he's had the job of making us walk tall again. And he's done that job wonderfully well. Leeds have won the League championship, the Fairs Cup, the F.A. Cup, the League Cup . . . but there was grudging acceptance of some of those triumphs, in the past. And when we faltered and fell, as in the European Cup and the European Cup-winners Cup, as in the F.A. Cup final against Sunderland, plenty of folk were quick to say: 'That's it – Leeds are over the hill.'

There might even have been an odd time or two when the Leeds players were tempted to wonder . . . but Don Review saw to it that we never failed to grit our teeth and return to the fray the following season determined to rout the doubters. Last season was the pay-off . . . and this time out, NO ONE will doubt our quality.

I believe that Leeds faced up to their greatest crisis just over a year ago, after Sunderland had beaten us in the F.A. Cup final. We were down – and then came the speculation that Don Revie would be leaving. That really had us worried. But the boss decided that he still had a job to complete at Leeds, and he set the example for our efforts last season, when we went through so many matches to set a new record for an undefeated run, and pile up a massive points lead in the championship.

At Leeds, we are a family. It's one for all, and all for one. Gordon McQueen, for instance, will tell you how the lads helped him to feel at home straight away after he had joined us from St. Mirren. And despite an injury list which would have crippled lesser clubs, we carried on, demonstrating not just all-round ability and strength in depth, but tremendous team spirit. Yes, it's all been a team effort; yet every team must have a leader. I'm the leader on the field, but the real leader, the inspiration for us all, has been Don Revie.

I once asked for a transfer, soon after he had become manager. Hibernian were ready to pay £25,000 for me, and I would have jumped at the move. The boss dug in his heels, and said the price must be £30,000 – and the deal never materialised. Around that time, he must have been a bit fed-up of hearing my moans, but he never lost patience. And he instilled into all of us the necessity for similar patience, in our desire to be recognised as a great side.

Last season, we silenced the critics in the best possible manner – by playing football which pulled in the fans and won us tributes, as well as matches. We let our feet do the talking for us on the field, and other people do the talking for us off it. It was the kind of talk which added up to genuine admiration, and the words we heard and read were such sweet music to our ears. We had had our moments of glory, in previous seasons; we had also suffered our share of heartaches. But last season really did bring the pay-off, in every way. And this time out, we are prepared to go on to even greater things. For there is always another Everest to be conquered, in football.

# The INTERNATIONAL Front

I'm coming up to the half-century mark for international caps, and I can still vividly remember my first game for Scotland – it was against Spain at Hampden Park in 1965, and the result was a 0–0 draw. From that moment on, it became one of my ambitions to play for Scotland in the finals of the World Cup . . . and in the summer of 1974, I managed it, when we went to West Germany. I was proud to be the skipper of Scotland, and I was delighted that we had made it, at long last. Because we had been trying for so long.

Scotland reached the final stages of the competition in 1958, when they went to Sweden. Like the other home countries, we came unstuck – Northern Ireland were the ones who went furthest, and they had been the least-rated side of all. That blow to Scottish pride was followed by another one, four years later, when we came nowhere again. But we all hoped it would be third-time lucky when the 1966 World Cup was staged in England.

What happened to Scotland proved

to be an even bigger let-down, for I am still convinced in my own mind that we should have got through . . . yet we never even managed to qualify. We were drawn in our qualifying section against Italy, Poland and Finland. We defeated the Finnish side twice, we beat Italy at Hampden and lost away, and we went to Katowice and drew with the Poles, 1–1. The stage was set for a triumphant march across the Border . . . but it never materialised.

Hampden Park was a cauldron of Scottish fervour when the Poles came over. It was the night we were going to make sure of qualifying – but in the last six minutes of the game, the Poles scored two goals and once more we were right out of the action. We should have had the game well won, before Poland struck those killer blows, but we didn't. And it took me a long time to get over that. I knew just what the England lads – in particular, my Leeds teammate, Norman Hunter – felt like, when the Poles came to Wembley and walked off with a draw which saw them qualify,

101

and England knocked out, with the 1974 World Cup looming up.

Until last summer, the closest I had got to participating in the World Cup finals was as a spectator, although I did go to Mexico in 1970. I was chosen as a member of a Great Britain team, and we all went along to watch the world's stars

*The FIFA World Cup.*

in action. It saddened me that Scotland were not represented, once again, and I vowed to myself that when the 1974 tournament came along, we would be there, if Billy Bremner had anything to do with it.

Italy finished up winning their section, for the 1966 World Cup – and we Scots were choked, when they made such a mess of their chance. We knew we could have done so much better. In 1970, we had to overcome West Germany and Austria. They were the stumbling-blocks, not little Cyprus, whom we beat comfortably home and away. We beat Austria 2–1 at Hampden, lost 2–0 away; we drew 1–1 with West Germany at Hampden, lost 3–2 away. And West Germany, who finished up leading our group, put paid to England in Mexico. So, as I say, for us there was another four-year wait, just as England have had to face a four-year wait now until the 1978 World Cup in Argentina. For Scotland, the sun really shone on a dark night at Hampden Park when we scored a victory over Czechoslovakia and we knew then that, come what may, we hadn't made a mess of it again – WE WERE THERE.

Tommy Docherty started it, Willie Ormond carried on the job of steering us to the 1974 finals. And I might add that Scotland had had a few team managers, over the years ... Andy Beattie, Sir Matt Busby, Jock Stein, Bobby Brown. Some of the best in the game had sought to put Scotland's name on the World Cup map, and it wasn't for want of trying that things didn't work out. It wasn't an easy thing for Willie

Ormond, either, taking over from Tommy Docherty in mid-stream, as it were; but we made it.

So now I'd like to set the scene for you, by giving you the background to the world's greatest sporting competition . . . thirty-eight ties in twenty-five days, from the opening match on Thursday, June 13, to the final on Sunday, July 7. And believe you me, the Germans really had been thorough in their preparations.

For a start, a World Cup tournament takes a lot of money – and it costs a great deal of money to stage, as well. West Germany started a huge lottery, called the Gluckspirale. It began for the 1972 Olympics, and it carried on for the 1974 World Cup. During three years, up to the Olympics, the Gluckspirale raked in more than £67,000,000, and paid out almost £18,000,000 in prize money; and well before the World Cup action had got under way, there was £3,000,000 in the kitty to start things off. Vouchers for World Cup tickets went on sale as long ago as April, 1973, at more than 200 agencies – and the vouchers for all the matches involving West Germany, the host nation, and Brazil, the holders, plus the final match, had been snapped up inside a couple of hours! Apart from that, it was estimated that almost half a million tickets would be sold outside West Germany, and that the final 'take' for the 1974 World Cup would amount to a world record.

There were nine stadiums for the games – in West Berlin, Hamburg, Hanover, Gelsenkirchen, Dortmund, Dusseldorf, Stuttgart, Frankfurt and Munich. Frankfurt had the honour of staging the first match, on June 13, and Munich was the venue for the final. Each stadium had an electronic scoreboard, parking facilities for at least 15,000 cars and 1,000 coaches . . . and landing space for crowd-control helicopters. Each ground had to be able to accommodate at least 1,200 reporters – from all over the world – and while the grounds in Munich and Berlin were up to Olympic standard, the other seven were either rebuilt, or built from scratch . . . at a total cost of £50,000,000

Provision had been made for total crowds of almost 2,500,000 at the thirty-eight ties, and with tickets priced at between £1·65 and £13·30 – yes, £13·30 – the fans would be forking out around £7,500,000, while the sale of television rights around the world was bringing in another £3,000,000. Does your mind begin to boggle at all these huge figures? Maybe . . . but it just goes to show what staging a World Cup tournament means in terms of cash and crowds. And, of course, above all, it shows exactly what tremendous interest there is in the World Cup.

For the start of the competition, there was a parade of all the sixteen competing nations, a real fanfare of colour and excitement. Brazil, the World Cup champions with three successes behind them, had the honour of kicking off in the first match, which was the only one to start at 5 p.m. . . . after the two-hour-long opening display. Incidentally, the grass for every one of the nine pitches had been imported especially from Holland, and each stadium had a World

Cup try-out with a big game before the tournament swung into action.

The sixteen teams were divided into four groups, each side coming up against the other, as in League matches. The top two teams in each group then went forward, and again they were split into two sections of four, with the 'league' system in operation once more. And the winners of the groups met in the final, with the runners-up playing off for third and fourth place. Only in the final and the game to decide third and fourth place was extra time allowed . . . and, just in case, the ruling was that if the final itself were drawn, after extra time, then there had to be a replay.

The first three countries to qualify were West Germany, as the host nation, Brazil, as the holders of the trophy, and Uruguay, who had qualified by winning their group on goal difference. Soon, Scotland had joined the ranks of the qualifiers, and so had Poland, Italy, Bulgaria . . . and one or two so-called no-hopers, such as Australia and Zaire. When the draw was made for the matches, Scotland were paired against Zaire, Brazil and the winners of a play-off between Yugoslavia and Spain. In the event, it turned out that the Yugoslavs got through, and so there we were – with our first game scheduled against Zaire. Oh, yes, I forgot to add that there was another unknown quantity in this competition . . . by the name of Haiti.

So, at long last, we all knew exactly where we stood, after the worry about getting through the qualifying rounds, and wondering whom we would be facing when we finally did get to West Germany. And I think you'll agree with me that getting to the finals of the World Cup competition is a tremendously exciting thing for the players concerned. For me, the honour of leading out Scotland in the 1974 World Cup will remain a vivid memory as long as I live. I was thrilled and proud to be Scotland's captain.

It's history now, of course, how Scotland fared in the World Cup, and I imagine that most of you watched the games on television. As usual, the tournament produced its heroes, its highlights and its low moments; but speaking for myself, I can only say that I'll never forget my trip to West Germany. It was hard going, because we were not there on holiday, and it was football, football all the time. Yet I wouldn't have missed it for the world, and not only did it add to my experience it gave me another glimpse of some of the greatest players in the game, from all over the world.

I am not easily impressed, when it comes to making judgments of my fellow professionals, and I don't always agree with the majority, when it comes to voting a player as being great. I'm prepared to accept from the old-timers that there were some truly great players in the past, and that they could still have made their mark in the game as we know it today. But I think you might find it interesting if I devote some space now to some of the footballers who I really feel have graced the game, during my time, and who have every right to be recognised as world-class, in every sense of the word.

# SIX OF THE BEST!

Through the years, a great many players have had fame thrust upon them, in the sense that people have called them great footballers. Well, I'll tell you something straight from the shoulder: I'm not easily impressed, when it comes to bestowing the label of greatness on players. Perhaps I am hard to please . . . but when I single out a man as a great footballer, then he's had to earn this recognition, so far as I'm concerned. And I'll go so far as to say that even Pele didn't measure up to my requirements for quite some time!

The 1974 World Cup tournament threw up some new names, and in spite of my being hard to please, I have to concede that the cream of the world's footballing nations was on parade, as sixteen countries battled away for the trophy and the right to be called the No. 1 Soccer nation in the world. Yet, at the end of it all, when I sit down to compile my list of the top six players, I have to say that some of them were not even there for the 1974 World Cup. One of them had already retired, to go into management; another is due to hang up his boots any time now. And still I could not dismiss either of them from my list of greats. So take a bow, Bobby Charlton and Edson Arantes do Nascimento – otherwise known as Pele. Yes, he is on my list now, all right.

Bobby Charlton – what can you say about him that hasn't already been said? Elsewhere in this book, we have taken a pretty close look at him, and at his brother Jack, who was one of my Leeds United team-mates for such a long time. So I'll say simply that Bobby Charlton, who collected no fewer than 106 international caps for England, and who scored 199 League goals for Manchester United, never ceased to impress me during his career as a player.

He had style, he had grace. He packed an explosive shot, even if he seldom headed a goal. He could make the ball do the work, when he was playing in midfield . . . and I'm like a lot of other people, when I say that neither England nor Manchester United have found it easy to replace him. Maybe with a vintage Bobby Charlton in their side, England would have qualified for the 1974 World Cup . . . maybe with a vintage Bobby Charlton in their side, Manchester United would not have struggled so desperately against relegation.

I've had plenty of praise myself, in the past year or so, but I've always been conscious of the fact that one man never made a team, and I've never forgotten that at Leeds United we have been a team, in every sense of the word. So, while repeating that one man, including Bobby Charlton, never made a team, let me add that Bobby's departure from the Manchester United and England scenes left awful gaps.

In a way, Bobby was a boy wonder – overnight, he grew to manhood after the Munich crash. And in a different way, Pele was another player who sprang swiftly to fame, for it was in the 1958 World Cup that Brazil launched him, as an unknown 17-year-old. He had become a regular first-teamer with Santos, and he scored the first time he played for Brazil – in a game against Argentina in Buenos Aires. Argentina were 1–0 ahead, and Pele was a substitute for Brazil. The coach sent him on, with instructions to 'get me a goal' . . . and Pele did. Three days later, Pele was scoring for Brazil again, in the 220,000-capacity Maracana stadium in Rio de Janeiro; and the week after that, he was among the twenty-two players named for the 1958 World Cup squad going to Sweden.

Pele had been taken along for the ride, really, but after having beaten Austria 3–0, Brazil could manage only a 0–0 draw against England, and this meant they had to win against Russia, to qualify for the quarter-finals. Brazil's team bosses sat up half the night, deliberating what to do. In the end, they chose Pele at inside-left, and Garrincha (who had only recently had an operation for appendicitis) on the right wing. Garrincha gave the Russian back a chasing, and Pele scored the second of Brazil's goals, in a 2–0 triumph.

In the quarter-final, Brazil were up against Wales, and it was stalemate, with 15 minutes to go. The Welsh had fought like tigers, never mind dragons, and Pele was tightly marked by Mel Charles, when he collected a pass from Nilton Santos. Charles went into the tackle, Pele drew back the ball with the sole of his boot, and flicked the ball into the air . . . and, as 'keeper Jack Kelsey rushed out to challenge, Pele lobbed the ball high over his head. The ball bounced on the empty goal line, and went into the net. And if you were watching the 1970 World Cup on television, you'll probably remember Pele trying to score a similar cheeky goal, but from a much longer distance, when he looked up and saw the 'keeper had come off his line. He almost did it, too.

Against France, when Brazil were 2–1 ahead, Pele broke away to clinch matters with three goals in twenty-three minutes, and that put Brazil into the final against Sweden. Brazil took a 2–1 lead, but it was still anyone's game – until Pele raced to meet a centre from the left. He leaped high into the air, controlled the ball with his chest, let the ball drop to his right thigh – and from there, flicked it over a defender's head. He raced round the man, beat another defender, and volleyed the ball past the 'keeper. Sweden scored a second goal, but Brazil totalled five ... and Pele struck home the fifth, with a header. In 10 days, Pele had scored seven goals, during four vital matches in the toughest competition in the world. And so the player who had been born on October 21, 1940, and hailed from a tiny mining town, became a world-famous figure in football.

Real Madrid made a £220,000 offer for him; Inter-Milan went up to £300,000; Roma were ready to bid £550,000. But Pele stayed with Santos. Money just couldn't buy him. He goes out of the game having scored more than 1,000 goals and having helped Brazil to three World Cup successes.

And although he made little impact in the 1966 World Cup in England, when he played although he was far from fit, I really came to appreciate his wonderful all-round ability during the 1970 World Cup in Mexico. It grieved me that I wasn't there playing for Scotland; instead, I had been named in a Great Britain side, and we were there as spectators. And when 1974 came around I was playing for Scotland, and Pele was no longer in the Brazilian side. But in spite of my early doubts about the wizardry of this man, I finally joined the legion of those who said he was truly great, and I couldn't have missed him out of my list, just as I couldn't have omitted Bobby Charlton. The 1974 World Cup competition had some big names, but it would have been even more magical, had Bobby and Pele been in their prime, and there to grace the occasion.

Another world-famous figure was missing, too: Eusebio, of Portugal, who did not qualify. And here again. I have to say that for me, this fellow earned the right to be called a great player. Remember how North Korea scored three times to rock Portugal at Goodison Park in 1966 – and how Eusebio scored four goals to inspire his side to a 5–3 victory? Remember, too, that great semi-final between England and Portugal?

I remember, also, a wet and windy night at Stoke-on-Trent, last season, when Eusebio played – and so did Bobby Charlton – in Gordon Banks's testimonial game. Eusebio was hampered by a leg injury, which didn't allow him to flex the knee fully; but he still showed what a marvellous footballer he could be, with his uncanny instinct for running into space, and his shooting and heading ability. The 1974 World Cup tournament was somewhat the poorer for the fact that another glittering star of world football was missing from the stage. But, again, he is close to the top of my personal list.

And now I come to the men who did make the World Cup in 1974. If you want to know who tops my list of

*Johann Cruyff . . . the man who tops Billy Bremner's list of world aces. Cruyff, once a star with Ajax Amsterdam, as well as Holland, now plays for Barcelona.*

current stars, there can be only one answer ... Johann Cruyff, lately of Ajax Amsterdam and now of Barcelona, in Spain. It needed nothing less than a one-million-pound transfer deal to persuade Ajax to part with Cruyff. And what a tremendous job he did for Barcelona!

In Spain, they soon came to idolise 'The Flying Dutchman'. Barcelona had been going through a very sticky time, and even when they signed Cruyff, many people thought that the Spanish club had made a £1M mistake. Barcelona were one of the best-supported clubs throughout Europe, with gates of around 65,000; but the sort of money which had been spent on signing Cruyff required a fantastic return, to give Barcelona full value. And they got it!

Barcelona played Malaga, and 98,000 people flocked to watch them. They played Spanish champions Atletico Madrid, and there was a 110,000 crowd. And the man behind it all was Cruyff. He lifted Barcelona from the doldrums, spearheaded their greatest-ever success over Real Madrid (a 5–0 victory), and took Barcelona to the top of the table, where they looked a surefire bet to win their first championship in fourteen years.

It was a different tale, indeed, from that of Real Madrid, who had expended around £300,000 on West Germany's midfield man, Gunter Netzer. Class player though he had been with Borussia Moenchengladbach, Netzer didn't find it so easy to turn it on for Real, as they languished down the table, and both club and player found it a bit of a struggle, in spite of Netzer's undoubted talents.

Now don't get me wrong. Netzer for me has a great deal of skill, but I feel at times he doesn't always seem to be in the mood to produce it. He is powerfully built, and he can mastermind the midfield. He also has a terrific shot, and can score goals. Cruyff, on the other hand, looks more slightly built, and you could be forgiven for wondering if this fellow would stand up to the treatment strikers often receive in their opponents' penalty area. But Cruyff reminds me in so many ways of Jimmy Greaves, when he was ghosting in for goals. Cruyff can play football like a dream; he has the skill and the positional sense to find space for himself, in the tightest situation and he always seems to be on the spot when there is a scoring chance to be taken. With Ajax, Cruyff was very much a part of the furniture – he had players around him who knew exactly what he wanted, in the way of service; and he knew their moves, as well. When he went to Barcelona, he had to show that he could maintain his form, and settle in with new team-mates. He did this with such success that he became a hero in Spain in a very short time, and in so doing, he proved that he was truly great. A world-class player in every way.

In his first League appearance for Barcelona, Cruyff scored two magnificent goals, so he was off to a good start. But he was more than a flash in the pan, as he continued to show dazzling form.

I often consider, in assessing players, whether or not they would survive in British football – not just survive, when

*Franz Beckenbauer of West Germany.*

we're playing in varying conditions such as on bone-hard grounds, on mudheaps of pitches, occasionally on ice and snow, but actually manage to emerge as stars. I think Netzer might accomplish this, providing he were dedicated enough; I'm certain that Cruyff would be able to adapt himself to soccer, British style.

Not only is he so skilled, but he is prepared to accept that there is a physical side to the game. He'll go in where angels might fear to tread, he'll win the ball in the air, and when an opponent has the ball, then he'll have a go at winning it off him. And in addition to all this, of course, he has that wonderful knack of being on the right spot at the right time to take scoring chances – and he's accurate enough to stick the ball in the net.

My next great player is another whom I feel would acquit himself well in our game ... West Germany's Franz Beckenbauer, of Bayern Munich. Beckenbauer is an elegant sort of a player – but make no mistake, he takes some stopping. He can play as a sweeper, in midfield ... or go boring through on a run which ends in a powerful shot. Just now and again, I feel, he tries to play it too coolly, when he's under pressure in defence; but he has such skills that most times he plays himself out of trouble – even if he's played himself into it, first.

Just before the 1970 World Cup, Beckenbauer was named as one of their all-time world XI by a panel of international sportswriters. He had played against England in 1966, he played in Mexico, and he made it a third time in West Germany. To the Bayern fans, he has long been known as 'King Franz', and he has won medals galore. Apart from his swift strikes from midfield, culminating in that power-packed shot, he is skilled at taking free-kicks and can fool defences with them. Maybe he won't be there, the next time around ... but as of now, he has certainly made a very real impact on the world football scene, and I happily include him in my lists of great players.

One of the most-honoured players in Italian football has been Gianni Rivera, nick-named the 'golden boy' when he first came into international prominence. Rivera is now around the thirty mark, but he has made his presence felt in international football, and as a midfield player myself, I have been able to stand back and admire his skills with the interest of a fellow-professional. A few years ago, Rivera was selected by European sports editors as the continent's No. 1 player, and – like Franz Beckenbauer – he has won honours galore with his club, A.C. Milan, as well as at international level. Like Beckenbauer, also, he has been a formidable World Cup opponent, and his keen soccer brain has conjured up many openings for Italy's strikers ... while he himself has shown that he can go forward, when the occasion demands this.

I've scored a few goals in my time, and I firmly believe that this is part of a midfield player's job. It calls for the ability to be quick, both mentally and physically. You've got to have the mental eye to spot an opening for a pass which can catch defences flat-footed,

111

you have to be physically quick, to control the ball and move it accurately, and you have to have a sharp eye for the chance to score a goal, as well as to make one. Beckenbauer's, as I have said, is a sort of elegant skill; Rivera has glided into positions, and he's made the move before you're aware of it, often enough.

I wouldn't claim that the players I have named are the only truly great players who have been on the world soccer stage, but I would argue with anyone that it's difficult to find half a dozen better. Certainly, in my career at the top, and in my experience of the World Cup football scene, these are the men I have come to admire most over the years. And sometimes I just wish that we could all have played in the same team, if only for 90 minutes . . . I think we would have given the opposition something to think about, don't you?

*Gianni Rivera of Italy.*

# GREAT SCOTS

Glasgow Celtic have been the most successful Scottish club in modern times, so it comes as no surprise when Celtic have three or four players in a Scotland team. Several of my international colleagues have graduated at Parkhead, under Jock Stein – players such as Kenny Dalglish, Danny Mc-Grain, George Connolly and Davie Hay Not to mention goalkeeper Alistair Hunter, and a player who was transferred from Celtic to Manchester United . . . Lou Macari.

For years, there seemed to be a prejudice north of the border about choosing 'Anglos' – players who had been transferred to English clubs – for the Scotland international team. I'm happy to say that that prejudice has been banished during the past two or three years – for good, I hope. I'm as fervent a Scot as the next one, but when we were striving to qualify for Munich, I didn't care whether a player came from north or south of the border, just so long as he could do his stuff in the Scotland team. And I was proud to lead the 'Anglos', as well as the home-based Scots, into the World Cup finals.

I've mentioned the star players of the world, in another article – Bobby Charlton, Pele, Eusebio, Cruyff, Beckenbauer and Rivera – and now I'd like to tell you something about a few of my own 'clansmen'. We've got centre-half Gordon McQueen at Leeds, of course, and it could be that within the next season or two quite a battle will develop between him and big Jim Holton, of Manchester United, for the No. 5 spot in Scotland's side. I can tell you that in the build-up to the 1974 World Cup, Gordon was as enthusiastic as anybody about big Jim's right to the centre-half jersey in Scotland's team, and I'll vouch for Jim Holton's ability, courage and will to win.

Jim's story is a fairy-tale one, because

113

he left Scotland to seek fame in English football – and finished up by being given a free transfer by West Brom. Harry Gregg, manager of Shrewsbury Town at the time, signed Jim, and within a matter of months he had moved on to Manchester United for an £80,000 fee. How's that for a rapid change in fortunes?

Jim went to Old Trafford at a bad time, for United were struggling to avoid relegation to the Second Division. Some folk reckoned that he was a bit rough on opponents; but he'll do for me, all right. A centre-half's job is to stop 'em scoring goals. And big Jim certainly proved an effective barrier down the middle of the field. He is robust, he is enthusiastic . . . but he's not deliberately dirty. Don't forget that Jim had to be pitched into a side struggling for First Division survival, and it must have been a tremendous responsibility on his shoulders, for he was still trying to gain experience. Off the field, this young giant of a footballer has a gentle smile and a quiet voice; he's an exceptionally nice lad. On the park, he tries to do his job as effectively as he knows how. That's what he's being paid for, and believe me, he earns his money.

There was another player whose name was often in the headlines last season, too – Denis Law. And this fellow is one of the supreme professionals in the game, take it from me. He made an international comeback at thirty-three and celebrated his thirty-fourth birthday with a trip to the League Cup final as a Manchester City player . . . and then going to the World Cup just a few months later. Yet he had been handed a free transfer by Manchester United at the end of the previous season.

Denis is a player after my own heart. He goes in where angels fear to tread, and he has taken plenty of knocks in his time, when scoring goals that were never really 'on'. I have the utmost admiration for the way this fellow plays his football, and for his attitude to the game. He won just about every honour possible with Manchester United, he played in Italian football for a spell; and he signed up with Manchester City to make it a dazzling finale to his big-time career. And the final curtain hasn't come down for him yet!

The three qualities which put Denis Law in the true world-class bracket are his tremendous ability to get into a position where he can snatch a goal; his bravery, because sometimes that scoring position is akin to being a 'suicide' slip fielder; and his absolute competitiveness. The years always take their toll in football, but nothing seems to have diminished Denis Law's sheer instinct for being where the action is, and his ability to direct a header or a shot into the net.

Kenny Dalglish is the kind of striker every manager would give a small fortune to sign. I remember one top English manager admitting, several seasons ago, when Kenny had only just burst upon the Scottish Soccer scene, that he would dearly love to be able to take him south of the border. But Kenny has stayed with Celtic, who know when they're on to a good thing, and although he's no giant, he has shown time and again that, like Denis Law, he has a nose for a scoring chance, and he can also set up chances for his team-mates. Like Denis – who so rarely wastes a pass – Kenny is one of my Scots for all seasons . . . a player who has achieved world-class stature, in my book.

And that brings me to Willie Morgan, who was signed by Manchester United from Burnley for close on £100,000 in 1968. Willie, who had joined the Turf Moor club in 1961, was regarded as a winger when he joined United, and he has had his ups and downs in football, for things didn't go too well for him at first, after he had left Burnley. With United, he played as a winger, but found that he wasn't clicking as he had done in his days at Turf Moor. Maybe he wasn't getting the same sort of service... whatever the reason, he had a bit of an in-and-out time.

Probably the changes in management didn't help him to feel settled either, but in the past couple of years, Willie has regained all his old zest for the game, especially since he switched to a midfield role. He is a tricky player on the ball, and he can take on one man after another and beat him. He has also shown that as a midfield player, he can spray the passes around for the benefit of his team-mates. I really believe that being chosen for Scotland helped Willie to regain both form and confidence, and since he became an international team-mate of mine, he has blossomed as one of the best. He's become an idol at Old Trafford, where he was made skipper last season, and rarely a week went by without him being the star performer in the team. That meant that in addition to ability, Willie Morgan had brought consistency into his game.

And so I come to another winger who made a switch to midfield – Tommy Hutchison, of Coventry City. Tommy signed for Blackpool when he left his first club in Scotland, and at around £10,000 he proved to be a bargain buy, indeed. Long and leggy, he soon became a favourite at Bloomfield Road, with his bewildering change of pace and his trickery as he went down the left wing, and it wasn't surprising when Coventry stepped in to give him a regular place in First Division football.

What did surprise many people was the fact that at the start of last season, Coventry team manager Gordon Milne switched 'Hutch' to a midfield role. Gordon explained that for one thing, Coventry were hit by injuries, and a key midfield man, Willie Carr – also a Scottish international – was out of action. Gordon believed that Tommy could take over a midfield role, and that he would have greater freedom in this position, and also be much more in the game. It wasn't long before Soccer was buzzing about 'Hutch', and I came to appreciate just what playing in midfield had added to his game, when he became a fully-fledged international. Tommy has years ahead of him at the top in football, and as he gains in experience I can only see him becoming even better. He has learned to 'read' situations in a game, and he knows when a pass is better than trying to take on a man and beat him. He also knows when he has the edge on an opponent, and in such circumstances he will go past the man as if he were not there, then cut in and slip a pass to a team-mate, or send over a dangerous cross from the wing.

By now, I reckon, you'll have got the impression that I'm a fan of the players I've mentioned in this article – and if so, you're dead right. To me, they are all players who have already given a great deal to the game in general, and to Scottish football in particular, at the highest level. And while some of them may be 'getting on a bit', others have the time in front of them to make an even greater impact.

I don't always see nothing but the white shirts of Leeds United. I can recognise ability, skill, courage and power in players with other teams. When they also play for Scotland, as international team-mates of mine, then I get to know them even better. And so far as I'm concerned, they've all got what it takes.

# ANSWERS TO QUIZ

1. The Harris brothers, who played for Chelsea in the 1967 F.A. Cup final.

2. Alex Dawson, in Manchester United's 5–3 win over Fulham in 1958.

3. Billy Bremner (Leeds), who made his debut alongside Don Revie.

4. Ray Wood (Manchester United), who was injured in the 1957 final against Aston Villa. His replacement, centre-half Jackie Blanchflower, conceded both goals.

5. Linfield, who dropped out of the F.A. Cup competition after only one game – a 2–2 draw with Nottingham Forest in 1888.

6. The referee was the famous Alf Bond, who had only one arm.

7. He's Ted MacDougall, now with Norwich.

8. He scored nine goals for Bournemouth against Margate in an F.A. Cup-tie in season 1971–72.

9. Gordon Banks won seventy-three England caps.

10. Antonio Carvajal, the famous Mexican goalkeeper.

11. Hungary, Austria, Sweden, West Germany and, for good measure, Italy last season.

12. Preston (1889), Aston Villa (1897) Tottenham (1961), Arsenal (1971).

13. When Hungary defeated England 7–1 in 1953.

14. Bill Perry (Blackpool), capped three times by England in season 1956–57.

15. Colin Viljoen (Ipswich Town).

16. Newcastle United (11 finals).

17. Ayresome Park, home of Middlesbrough, who were then in Division 3.

18. Tottenham, who were in the Southern League when they won the F.A. Cup in 1901.

19. Doncaster Rovers, who were 92nd in the League when they played at Liverpool.

20. George Male, who made his

117

debut for Arsenal in the 1930 F.A. Cup final.

**21.** Manchester United (the Munich disaster).

**22.** Torino, who lost 18 players in an air crash at Superga, Italy, in 1949.

**23.** Blackburn Rovers (1890) and Bury (1903).

**24.** Denis Law, who scored six goals for Manchester City in an F.A. Cup-tie against Luton ... which was then abandoned.

**25.** In 1965, when Manchester United pipped Leeds for the title.

**26.** West Brom, in 1931, won the F.A. Cup and promotion.

**27.** Liverpool, champions and U.E.F.A. Cup winners in season 1972–73.

**28.** Benfica, who have played twice in European Cup finals at Wembley.

**29.** Wilf Smith, who played at left-back for Sheffield Wednesday against Everton in the 1966 F.A. Cup final.

**30.** Believe it or not ... Leeds United, who lost sixteen consecutive F.A. Cup games from 1952 to 1963.

**31.** Tommy Gemmell and Len Chalmers.

**32.** Manchester United 4, Benfica 1.

**33.** Joe Mercer (Aston Villa, 1961, and Manchester City, 1970).

**34.** Ron Saunders (Norwich City and Manchester City).

**35.** Sir Alf Ramsey, then with Ipswich, who won the Third Division in 1957, the Second in 1961 and the First in 1962.

**36.** Bill Perry scored Blackpool's winner in the 1953 F.A. Cup final against Bolton. Blackpool won 4–3.

**37.** Bobby Murdoch, now with Middlesbrough, scored Glasgow Celtic's 6,000th League goal.

**38.** Sunderland (1973), Preston (1964) Leicester (1949) and Burnley (1947).

**39.** Millwall (1937), Port Vale (1954), York City (1955) and Norwich City (1959).

**40.** Johnny Giles, who up to last season had played in one F.A. Cup final for Manchester United and in five for Leeds, including the replay against Chelsea.

**41.** Moscow Dynamo.

**42.** Real Madrid.

**43.** Newcastle United and Exeter City.

**44.** Bristol City, Swindon Town, Wrexham and York City.

**45.** Charlton Athletic and Port Vale.

**46.** In Budapest, in Vienna and in Madrid.

**47.** Sunderland have won the League title six times.

**48.** Stoke won their first major trophy when they collected the Football League Cup.

**49.** Alun Evans became the first teenager transferred for £100,000 from one English club to another, when he went from Wolves to Liverpool.

**50.** Aston Villa and West Brom have been League Cup finalists three times each.

**51.** Villa beat Rotherham on a 3–2 aggregate, in season 1960–61.

**52.** The first 100,000 crowd for a League Cup final was in 1972.

**53.** Ralph Coates, Tottenham's substitute, scored the winner against Norwich in the 1973 League Cup final.

**54.** Arsenal were losing League Cup finalists in 1968 and 1969.

**55.** Manchester United were the first English club to compete in the European Cup.

**56.** Willie Carlin, who has played for Liverpool, Halifax, Carlisle, Sheffield United, Derby County, Leicester City, Notts. County, and Cardiff.

**57.** Alan Ashman managed the Greek club, Olympiakos.

**58.** West Brom beat Everton 1–0 in the 1968 F.A. Cup final.

**59.** West Brom lost the 1970 League Cup final, against Manchester City.

**60.** Alan Birchenall, who went from Sheffield United to Chelsea to Crystal Palace to Leicester City in deals totalling £300,000.

**61.** Bobby Charlton scored 199 League goals.

**62.** Bob Latchford cost £350,000 when he was signed by Everton from Birmingham, in February 1974. The package deal included two players (Kendall and Styles) and £80,000 cash.

**63.** Manchester City paid Motherwell £100,000 for goalkeeper Keith MacRae.

**64.** John Charles, Gerry Hitchens, Denis Law, Joe Baker and Jimmy Greaves.

**65.** Harry Gregg (Swansea) and Tony Waiters (Plymouth).

**66.** Eddie and Frankie Gray, of Leeds United.

**67.** Jimmy Greaves had scored 100 League goals by the time he was twenty years and nine months old.

**68.** Howard Kendall became the youngest F.A. Cup-finalist when he

played for Preston against West Ham, in 1964, twenty days before his eighteenth birthday.

**69.** Len Shackleton scored six goals on his debut for Newcastle.

**70.** Stanley Matthews, in 1947.

**71.** Stanley Matthews, Tom Finney and Danny Blanchflower.

**72.** Denis Law and Joe Baker both played for Torino.

**73.** Rodney Marsh began his League career with Fulham.

**74.** Wyn Davies, Welsh international, who has played for Bolton, Manchester City, Manchester United and Blackpool.

**75.** Ron Ashman.

**76.** Norwich won the Football League Cup in 1962, when they beat Rochdale on a 4–0 aggregate.

**77.** John Bond played for West Ham.

**78.** Pele was seventeen, when he played in the 1958 World Cup, in Sweden.

**79.** Jairzinho scored seven goals in the 1970 World Cup.

**80.** Colin Stein, now with Coventry, cost £100,000 when he moved from Hibernian to Glasgow Rangers.

**81.** Alf Common cost £1,000 when he was signed by Middlesbrough from Sunderland, in 1906.

**82.** Denis Law cost Manchester City a reputed £55,000, when they first signed him.

**83.** City signed Law from Huddersfield Town.

**84.** Italy and Uruguay had each won the World Cup twice.

**85.** West Germany had won the 1954 World Cup, in Switzerland.

**86.** Starting in 1930, the World Cup

has been staged in Uruguay, Italy, France, Brazil, Switzerland, Sweden, Chile, England, Mexico and West Germany.

**87.** Gunter Netzer played for Borussia Moenchengladbach.

**88.** Johann Cruyff joined Barcelona from Ajax.

**89.** Manchester United, who had three players voted European Footballer of the Year.

**90.** The players: Bobby Charlton, Denis Law and George Best.

**91.** Don Revie, who won the Manager of the Year award with Leeds, and the Footballer of the Year award with Manchester City.

**92.** Bill and Bob Shankly, Ted and Benny Fenton, and Jack and Bobby Charlton.

**93.** England's best placing in the European Nations Cup was in 1968, when they came third, after Italy and Yugoslavia.

**94.** No country has won the Nations Cup more than once, so far. The winners have been Russia, Spain, Italy and West Germany.

**95.** England played France.

**96.** France beat England, 5–2.